Pathways of SPIRITUAL
Awakening

Professional Woman Publishing
Prospect, Kentucky

Pathways of Spiritual Awakening
Copyright 2021 © Unity of Sarasota
All rights reserved.

Published by: Unity of Sarasota
office@unityofsarasota.com

Publishing Consultant: Professional Woman Publishing, LLC
www.pwnbooks.com

ISBN 13: 978-0-578-24357-3

Printed in the United States of America

DEDICATION

Dedicated to you, along your journey of spiritual awakening and transformation.

UNITY OF SARASOTA
2020 BOOK PROJECT

*We are grateful for the financial support of Unity of Sarasota's
Book 2020 Project; Pathways of Spiritual Awakening:
Uplifting Stories of Personal Transformation.
Peg Beck
Glenn and Kathy Boston
Donna Day
Julie Donnelly
Jennifer Johnston
Dr. Debra Sandberg
Rev. Dr. Suzi Schadle
Jerry Stricker*

*We are grateful to Rev. Dr. Suzi Schadle, Sr. Minister, Unity of Sarasota
for the spiritual idea for this creative collaboration and appreciate the
dedication of our Publisher, Linda Ellis Eastman of PWN Publishing,
designers, and editorial staff.
We appreciate the co-authors who have shared their
stories of spiritual inspiration.*

*Unity of Sarasota 2020 Book Project Editorial Board/Reviewers
Dr. Michael A. Lindquist (Chair)
Madelyn Balitz
Peg Beck
Dr. Kim Mae Johnson
Rev. Dr. Suzi Schadle*

INTRODUCTION

Pathways of Spiritual Awakening: Uplifting Stories of Personal Transformation features stories which will uplift and inspire you to navigate life's challenges. These are true personal accounts about each author's journey through a difficult life experience and how that experience has transformed their lives and brought peace to those who were suffering the emotions of fear, despair, anxiety, guilt…. These stories creatively explore how to use universal spiritual principles of empowering and life-affirming practical spirituality for richer living.

The authors come from various backgrounds and experiences. Some experienced grief at the loss of a loved one, others turned away from God and relied on drugs and alcohol for solace and comfort. Many of the writers reflect on confusion, exhaustion, and despair brought on by life-changing experiences, which ultimately became opportunities for awakening.

Some authors chose to use newfound wisdom to guide their life, while another learned that love only comes when you learn to love yourself.

Often, what is most personal is also most universal. Our hope is that these personal stories resonate with you, and you find insights that are helpful for your own life's journey.

If you desire to grow and experience new levels of spiritual awakening and personal growth, and you hunger for greater understanding of the Spirit within, then these stories may provide you with the inspiration to nourish your soul.

We are sure these stories will support you on your spiritual journey in a closer relationship with the God of your understanding.

And together we say, Thank God Within and All Around Us. Blessings on Your Journey

TABLE OF CONTENTS

1. God's Meaning of Forgiveness   3
   Dr. Kim Mae Johnson

2. CHOICES: Anxiety and Fear During Difficult Times   13
   Dr. Michael A. Lindquist

3. Unexpected Change:
   A Catalyst for Spiritual Transformation   23
   Peg Beck

4. The Day I Stopped Being A Fool   39
   Rev. Dr. Suzi Schadle

5. It's All About Perspective   53
   Betty Mann McQueen

6. Intuition, The Voice of God   73
   Jenny Johnson

7. Taking the Leap   83
   Jennifer "Revel" Johnston

8. Thanksgiving   91
   Caroline Robertie

9. How I Overcame, Survived, and Learned to
   Have Peace With the Passing of My Daughter, Kim   101
   Jerry Stricker

TABLE OF CONTENTS

10. Finding God During the Darkest Days of My Life   111
    Julie Donnelly

11. Solitude vs. Loneliness   119
    Madelyn Balitz

12. The Greatest Gift to Us is Never Saying Goodbye   131
    Julie Cook Downing

13. The Mermaid's Emergence   143
    Kaileia Kostroun

14. My Inspiration   155
    Susan Perry

15. Leaning Into Grief – The First Year   163
    Lisa Arundale

16. Higher Love   173
    Ginger Wilson

17. The Gift of Aging   183
    Laurel D. Rund

Pathways of SPIRITUAL Awakening

ABOUT THE AUTHOR

Dr. Kim Mae Johnson

Dr. Kim Mae Johnson is a college professor with 36 years' experience in the field of English Second Language learning and acquisition. She is a writer, inspirational speaker, and lecturer.

She is an ordained interfaith minister and spiritual advisor. She holds a master's degree and a doctoral degree in education. She has recently finished writing her first book on the power of the mind. She currently resides in Canada where she is also a businesswoman. She continues to do writing and research on spirituality.

ONE

God's Meaning of Forgiveness

By Dr. Kim Mae Johnson

When the local college that I attended in North America offered a two-month exchange program to the Caribbean, I knew it would be an exciting opportunity for me. I was a young adult exploring the world. I was not sure what I wanted to do in life, but I was ready for adventure.

Coming from a family of seven children, we went to church every Sunday, ate our meals together, and lived modestly. No one in the family had ever really travelled much. So, when I had the chance to study abroad for half a semester, I eagerly accepted.

There were eight students and a counsellor who came from overseas at the end of August for a period of two months. They each lived in a family with their counterparts experiencing the North American culture. My family and I had the privilege of welcoming a Christian girl, Cheryl, into our home for the duration of the visit. She was an outgoing person with a friendly and flirtatious smile. We learned about her country and her values. I remember one evening she showed me her Bible that she kept by her bedside. We shared a common faith.

Towards the end of October, I was among the eight North American students who accompanied the exchange students back to the Caribbean. I was billeted with another family since the living quarters were in proximity of the community college. Nevertheless, I saw Cheryl for common activities, classes, and excursions.

Three weeks into the exchange, while on a field trip at the beach, I was sexually attacked by one of the exchange students from overseas. He stole my innocence and shattered my world. I remember praying to God to spare me my life, although perhaps, I should not have muttered a word. My life no longer had any meaning for me.

Even though I was with a group of 16 students who were all participants in the program, I felt so alone. There was no one I could talk to who would be able to right the wrong. I was ashamed. I was terrified. There were so many "What if" questions that filled my mind. What if I saw the rapist again? What if he tried to attack me yet another time? What if I became pregnant?

One of the teachers at the college overseas was Alexander. He was from the United Kingdom and taught chemistry. He was a fine young man just out of university and not much older than me. He seemed to relate well to the students. He was handsome and soft spoken.

Alexander expressed an interest in me and my feelings for him were mutual. Since I was a student, he conducted himself professionally and we became more acquainted with each other.

He participated in some of the student activities and accompanied us on field trips. He seemed to enjoy being with the young expats and learning about other countries and cultures.

One event Alexander attended was a community supper where he sat beside me. As we were talking about life in general, Alex expressed his desire to enter into the ministry. He had showed me a Bible of his that was marked with notes in red ink. I was appalled that he dared deface his Holy book like that!

Alexander was able to make me smile again. He showed me what young love was supposed to be like. His words were soft and his touch was tender. Our values and beliefs intertwined. We were in sync in so many ways, but deep in my heart, I knew it could not work.

Since Alexander had expressed an interest in the ministry, I reasoned that he would want a chaste woman; that I was not. I was tarnished. I was tainted. I was not that pure woman I felt he would have wanted and most certainly deserved. So, I kept the attack a secret. I could not bring myself to tell Alex that I had been raped.

I had to return to North America in late December. It was heartbreaking not knowing when I would see Alex again. We promised to stay in contact, and we did. A year later, he moved back to the United Kingdom to pursue his studies and we continued our correspondence for a few years afterwards.

I was a university student when Alexander received his calling to go into the ministry.

We were both on marginal budgets and following differing paths, so our prospects of meeting were close to nil. With technology being what it was in the early 1980s, our main source of communication was mail. Telephone calls were once a year due to the exorbitant rates. We sent each other pictures and love letters, but the relationship could not survive the 3,000-mile distance across the Atlantic Ocean.

Alexander ended our relationship and I drowned myself in sorrow and tears.

We went our own ways. I sought Alex in the men I dated, but to no avail. After failed relationships and a divorce, I wrote to Alexander at the last address I had known dating back five years. I was hoping that perhaps there would be the remote chance that he would still want to see me, but I was wrong. I could not have been more mistaken. He replied, but not with the loving words that were indicative of his nature. He had gone into the ministry and was now married. He penned that, for him, our love was just fond memories.

I ached. I cried. My heart died that day.

I looked for Alex in subsequent relationships. I had two children and even pondered naming one Alexander, so that he would be in my life forever. I felt robbed of the love for which I yearned. I thought every man was a potential Alexander only to be disappointed by hardship, disappointment, and abuse. If love was supposed to be tender, kind, giving, and compassionate, why was I not finding it?

I continued my quest for the perfect love. In each relationship, I looked for the gentle nature of Alex, but never found it. I then met a retired science teacher and was in a relationship with him for eight years. Due to complications resulting from alcoholism, he became very ill and passed away at home in my arms. It was devastating to hear him gasp for his last breath of life and feel his heartbeat for his final moment with me.

Years after the death of my partner, I was again searching for the answers to the questions that had haunted me. I started to attend services at a beautiful chapel on the outskirts of the city. I became acquainted with the clergy who ran the sanctuary. The pastoral coordinator got me involved with the conferences and events that were held there. She wanted me to participate in a one-week retreat.

Without asking too many questions, I agreed. The topic of the retreat was forgiveness.

I followed the sermons and services of the week. One member of the clergy, Father Christian, gave a talk about how it was important to forgive when someone wronged you. He explained how he had counselled a gentleman whose wife had been murdered. The Father had listened to how the man's life was in shambles and the killer incarcerated. The Father gently spoke to the man about the power of forgiveness. He closed his lecture leaving my questioning mind filled with grief and resentment.

Forgive? Why? Why should the man forgive the killer? The man did nothing wrong, nor did I when I was attacked many years ago. I kept wondering why we had to forgive. Why should we pardon the killer and the rapist? Why are victims supposed to forgive when they are not at fault? This made absolutely no sense to me. The idea was preposterous, and I did not want to be a part of any of that.

The following evening, there was a healing service at the chapel. I attended. Again, it was about forgiveness. Then, each person met with two counsellors for the laying on of hands. The two people I met were the pastoral coordinator and Father Michel. They asked me how I wanted to be healed. In tears, I told them about the assault. I questioned how they could ask me to forgive the rapist. I strongly told them that I could not do it. I bowed my head in shame.

Father Michel put his hand on my chin and said, "When you are down, look up. Look up to God the Father." He explained to me that I had it all wrong that the forgiving was for me and not the assailant. I asked why I should forgive myself. He explained that forgiveness was not about forgiving the other person or justifying his behavior. It meant letting go the resentment and hatred harbored inside me so that it would not harden my heart. It was about letting go so that the perpetrator could no longer control my thoughts, words, or actions. The forgiveness was for me so that I could heal the inflicted wounds. In God's eyes, I was still His pure child.

Father Michel's words soothed and enlightened me. This encounter allowed me to open up and talk about the assault 37 years after the attack. I no longer had to carry the burdened feelings of guilt and shame. I could be free from the bonds that had tied me down and rendered me mute for so long. I would perhaps be relieved from the haunting and recurring nightmares.

Then, and only after Father Michel's explanation, did I finally understand what forgiveness truly meant.

After the autumn leaves had fallen and the winter snow had come and gone, spring settled in for a few months. With spring came Easter. On Good Friday, I went to the chapel to spend the afternoon in silence and reflection. I had a prayer request in mind. I jotted it down as so:

"O Lord my God, I ask on this Good Friday to meet a good Christian man who will love me for who I am and who I will love in return. I ask to be united in a long-term relationship leading to marriage. This I ask in the name of Jesus Christ the Son our Lord. Amen."

I figured that if I could not seem to pick the right man for me, that I would turn it over to God in prayer. If anyone could help me, it would be Him. I was vulnerable. I knew by making such a request that the person would be Divinely selected for me.

I lit a candle and spent the quiet afternoon in solitude sitting in the old stone chapel in prayer.

A couple weeks later, after arriving home in the evening from a class I had given, I checked my phone for messages. I received one on a social media site that I did not visit very often. I opened the message, and it was from a Reverend A. Forbes inquiring if I had been a participant in the exchange program at the community college in the Caribbean in the early 1980s. He was hunting down a memory and was wondering if I were the person in question.

My heart raced. I recognized that he was the Alexander I had met and fallen in love with so many years ago. I was thrilled that he had fulfilled his dream of becoming a minister. It made my heart sing. I had no idea why he was contacting me at this point in time. This was the first contact in nearly 30 years!

We corresponded through electronic mail and text messages. We wrote about our lives and our different journeys. I disclosed the attack to him. He was very sympathetic and understanding. We cried together. For years, Alexander had been searching for me to apologize and straighten things out, but he could never find me. He had his own painful story. He was now divorced and, as a clergyman, felt all the guilt and shame, albeit irrational and undeserved. We called and spoke face-to-face. We became a means of healing to each other. As we did, an old connection was remade.

After lengthy calls and hundreds of texts and letters, Alexander scheduled a flight to North America for study and to visit me. My heart was quivering with excitement. I had not seen him in so many years. On my way to the airport, my mind questioned, "What if he does not come off that flight?" "What if Alex has changed his mind?" "What if he does not want to see me after all?" My heart sank and rose as it died and was revived several times with flipflopping thoughts as to whether Alexander would actually appear in person instead of just virtually, as I had known him these past months.

I met Alexander at the airport. I arrived early so as not to miss a second of being with him. I recognized Alex as soon as he came through the gate. He whisked me in his arms as we spun around in a warm embrace. The heartfelt feelings of love and tenderness came gushing back to me.

We spent 16 precious days becoming reacquainted and reminiscing about our memories of yesteryears. We participated in choir, readings, devotions, and services together. He was warmly welcomed into my family. I will cherish those days forever. We took advantage of every moment by savoring it and never wanting to give it back, lest it be lost for another 37 years.

Alexander was a part of my past and present. Towards the end of his stay, he asked me to be a part of his future when he proposed to me.

Soon, Alex will move to North America where, with the will of God, he will occupy a vacancy at a local church. I will be honored to be his wife and to help him to serve in the ministry. When I call out to God in prayer, I am convinced that He will send His very best as He did by sending me Reverend Doctor Alexander Forbes. Thank you!

Notes:

ABOUT THE AUTHOR

Dr. Michael A. Lindquist

Michael grew up overseas, beginning school in England, moving to Panama, and graduating from High School in Seoul, Korea. Michael earned degrees from: Univ. of Tampa (BS), FIT (MS), and Argosy Univ. (EdD). He enlisted in the US Army and commissioned Second Lieutenant, Field Artillery. After 31 years of service he retired, served as Executive Director of the Congressional Medal of Honor Society; formed Adrian Consulting. Today, he teaches for Univ. of Phoenix. He has published academic articles, books of poetry and a series of Children's illustrated books. He is a member and Prayer Chaplain at Unity of Sarasota.

TWO

CHOICES:
Anxiety and Fear During Difficult Times

By Dr. Michael A. Lindquist

The sun rose over a typical September morning. The air was cool, a slight breeze blew in from the northwest. John awoke feeling anxious, dressed and went downstairs for breakfast with the rest of the family. John's mother greeted him with eyes red from crying; his sister looked up at him briefly and then looked away without saying a word.

"Have some breakfast" said John's mom. "I have made your favorites; pancakes and bacon, extra crisp."

Jenny, John's sister, looked at John again, this time with sadness and some fear showing in her youthful eyes.

"Are you really going to do it", she asked?

"Yea, I suppose I am. After all, what choices do I have" John replied?

Jenny spoke again. "My friend Terry, she told me they killed her cousin last week in Vietnam. He was the same age as you. She told me her aunt and uncle are unhappy, but also she told me her family was very proud too."

"Jenny, that's enough talk about someone dying" mom said as she looked soulfully at her son John. He was just eighteen and had only this past June graduated from High School with honors. He had his entire life in front of him and she would be damned if she were going to let him go off to some stupid, useless war that had no purpose other than satisfying some politician's whim.

John's dad come into the kitchen and announced, "It's time to go John. I have already put your gear in the car. Do you have your passport and the money I gave you?"

"Yes, sir" John replied.

His mother began to cry. "Write to us as soon as you get settled. Be sure to stay warm and don't worry about us." She continued to cry and hugged her son, wondering if she would ever see him again.

As John and his dad drove away, he looked back at his mother and sister and wondered, 'am I doing the right thing?' By day's end John was in Canada, a refuge for those who wanted to escape the draft and the consequences of war.

Across town, a similar morning was beginning. Michael was dressed and had eaten a nutritious breakfast. His dad, like Johns' dad, would drive him this morning, but the destination would be much different. Michael was on his way to the Military Enlistment Processing Center (MEPS). Later in the day he would raise his right hand and swear to defend the constitution of the United States of America.

Michael was a year older than John and had tried college. He spent the year majoring in drinking beer, playing cards and girls, leaving little time for his studies. When Michael returned home with a less than stellar GPA, his father had introduced him to the local Army recruiter. With the similar feelings of fear, trepidation, and anxiety to John's feelings, Michael drove away with his dad at the wheel of their old 1957 Mercury. This was the car in which he had learned to drive, the car in which he had taken Barbara to the Senior Prom, the car he had almost wrecked drag racing along Lonesome Point Road. He looked back at his mother as she waved goodbye and wondered, 'am I doing the right thing?'

This story presents observations and thoughts about people's reactions during tough times. It is also about the Nation's reaction to the Vietnam War and the reactions to the social injustices brought upon American minorities in the 21st Century.

Raised in a military family, I experienced travel across America and the world over. During my travels, I saw societies where there is no God; freedom is something that individuals cannot hope to have, and cultures with values different from my own do not enjoy the same liberties and economic prosperity that I enjoy as an American. Regardless of where I lived, I saw that it was American values that enable people to live their lives with social purpose, in happiness and for personal fulfillment.

American involvement in the war in Vietnam during the 1960s and early 1970s divided the country. Protests, including riots that brought destruction to our cities, were commonplace.

Today, protests are happening for different reasons. The story of the two young men facing the ethical and moral dilemmas of going to war raised questions of young American's. At the time, both these young men faced fear and displayed courage. Similar stories are being told today as American's, young and old, confront their own ethical dilemmas about equality and fairness here in America. They too are facing fears and displaying courage.

The Vietnam War was prior to the 'All-Volunteer Army" concept. The young men who were being required by law to be registered for the draft and, if drafted to be prepared to go to war, faced difficult choices. Each young man feared injury or death if they went to war or the consequences of imprisonment and/or being shunned by society for failing to meet every citizen's obligation to protect and defend American freedom and democracy.

The number of young men who were sent to fight in Vietnam was 2.5 million. Of that number 58,169 were killed and 304,000 were injured while in Vietnam. They estimated the number of those young Americans who went abroad in the late 1960s and early 70s to avoid serving in the war 100,000. Ninety percent went to Canada*

Richard M. Nixon was President of the United States, Melvin Laird had succeeded Robert McNamara as Secretary of Defense. Bob Dylan, Joan Baez and Peter, Paul & Mary sang of the horrors of war. The desire for peace was punctuated by, "It Better End Soon", by the group "Chicago" and "Mason Profitt's Band". "Two Hangmen", was a song that became an underground radio staple about the troubling direction the country was heading.

Throughout the United States, the mood toward the war had grown bitter. Families were divided between those who were behind the President and his actions and those who classified themselves as anti-war. Throughout the country, many young men were fulfilling their duty by joining the Military service. At the same time thousands of citizens were exercising their rights as a free people to speak out in protest to what they perceived as an unjust war.

One notable protest came at the 1968 Democratic National Convention in Chicago. Their antiwar demonstrators clashed with the police, and the images of police beating students shocked television audiences across the country and around the world. Another protest that caught the world's attention was Kent State University, May 4, 1970, where the Ohio National Guardsmen injured 13 students, killing four of them. These were not good times for Americans.

Today the President of the United States is facing similar challenges as those presented to President Nixon, reminiscent of the profound social upheaval of the 1960s. However, today's conflict is not caused by an unpopular war being fought by soldiers, rather disagreements between average citizens related to the social injustices served against minorities.

Throughout the United States the mood toward bias against minorities, police brutality and violence against women has grown angrier, dividing communities between those who are behind those who support the status quo and those who demand real reform. Throughout the country, thousands of citizens are exercising their rights as a free people to speak out in protest to what they perceive are the prevailing injustices. There are movements including Black Lives Matter, and Me Too that are dividing the country, pitting black against white, women against men that stoke the fires and are the catalyst for demonstrations.

In communities across the country, people are taking to the streets. The most notable protests to date have been in Minneapolis, Minnesota, resulting from the death of an African American by a white police officer. This incident, while centered in Minneapolis, gave way to over 1,700 separate demonstrations across all 50 states. Many of these protest demonstrations have become violent like those protest demonstrations of the 1960's.

With this as background, then and now, we turn our attention to the ethical dilemmas we all face and the associated fear and courage we all experience.

In 1968, I was the young man who faced the ethical dilemma, to fight in the war in Vietnam or avoid the draft by moving to Canada. I joined the U.S. Army and later fought in Vietnam (1969–1970).

While I feared injury or death, I believed that as an American; I had to defend freedom and fight for liberty of those who were having their freedoms taken from them. I knew that many of my peers, experiencing similar fears, were electing to avoid military service. I, like many of those who fought rather than flee, considered those who did not fulfill their obligation as American citizens to be cowards.

In 1982 I was teaching R.O.T.C at the University of Wisconsin–Whitewater and Milton College. One day I received an invitation from a local high school history teacher to come and speak to his students about the Vietnam War. This teacher was one who, as a young man, faced with the same decisions I had about military service. However, he made the choice to go to Canada rather than risk injury or death in Vietnam.

In speaking with the students, we both described how and why we decided as we did. We described our experiences during a time when the country was divided, much like today. I came away from that discussion with a new realization; we were both young men with similar fears. My values included "my country, right or wrong" while his values included "convictions about social justice and strong anti-war sentiment". With the values we held, we had different motivations, responsibility vs. injustice. These differences in values drove our decisions. While it took courage for me go to war, similarly it took courage for him to stand by his convictions of social justice.

Upon returning from Vietnam, I was spiritually bankrupt, however, my values of responsibility remained strong. Because of these held values, I made Military Service a career.

Today I believe:

- Decisions, made each day, are based upon the set of values I hold, based upon common beliefs and commitments to some level of ethical behavior.

- How I live my life is of greater importance than my own individual achievements.

We all face similar dilemmas. It is not about right or wrong, but about the values we hold. Those who value money and the accumulation of things, follow the mantra, 'at the end of life, he has the most toys wins'. They are comfortable in their lives and unwilling to see the injustices experienced by others for what they are. Those who value the rights of a free people to "Life, liberty and the pursuit of happiness" stand by their convictions. They support justice for everyone regardless of race, color, ethnicity, or sexual identity.

Fear of certain things that might confront us has developed over generations. We are adaptive because of our reactions to fear those things that might hurt us. Most psychologists recognize that it is the inherent fear, developed within humans, that keeps us safe. Our fear manifests itself when we are confronted by wiring of the brain that over time has taught us to be fearful.

Much like fear, courage is a part of the human make-up where the connections of the synopses of the brain determine if a person will act heroically. It takes courage to overcome our fears and phobias. Courage is characterized by an action taken for the purpose of achieving something noble and involves significant risk. Courage is often used interchangeably with other terms such as brave or heroic.

Today I hold these truths that define who I am:

I am an American. I value a higher power, one greater than myself. I value freedom; freedom to choose, freedom to move, freedom to fail and freedom to succeed, freedom to create, express, and communicate those beliefs, which are my own. I value family. Last, I value those individual characteristics that modern societies consider good.

I value God. I believe there is a God. My body will wither, and my soul will never die. To support this belief, I turn to Christian, Islamic and Buddhist writings; "I tell you the truth, he who believes has everlasting life" (John 6:47). "And Allah does not respite a soul when its appointed term has come, and Allah is Aware of what you do" (Koran 63.11). [After death], some are reborn in the womb; evildoers are born in hell; those who commit meritorious deeds go to heaven; and those who are free from worldly desires realize nirvana (CANTO VII, The Holy One, 126).

I value Freedom. Without freedom I am living another's beliefs; under someone else's ethical standards, not my own. Unconditional freedom exercises individual action without the regard to the consequences of those actions to oneself, others, or the world in which they live. We exercise conditional freedom within boundaries and constraints; those boundaries and constraints that guarantee that freedom expressed do not deny the freedoms of others. American freedom is conditional. America is a country whose first covenant is the rule of law. The rule of law is there to guarantee individuals their rights to life, liberty, and pursuit of happiness while protecting society.

I value Family. I believe we are obligated to one another; our family extends beyond our home, our community, our Nation and extends to all humankind.

I value honesty, integrity, and truth. I believe that without courage, candor, communication, commitment, and cooperation there can only be conflict, crisis, chaos, cowardice, and calamity.

I believe in America. I believe each of us has the obligation to exercise our individual responsibility to preserve the American way of life with determined resolve. I believe that without personal sacrifice future generations will not experience the freedoms and economic prosperity that we as a nation were once privileged to enjoy.

Today everyone should be encouraged to reevaluate our values as individuals and as a country. We will never be the men and women God created us to be until we can all conclude that living our lives in this Global community requires commitment to a set of ideals that embrace equality, justice, and diversity.

References

History.com. (2008). Statistics about the Vietnam War

http://www.vhfcn.org/stat.html#:~:text=One%20out%20of%20every%2010%20Americans%20who%20served,War%20II.%2075%2C000%20Vietnam%20veterans%20are%20severely%20disabled.

History.com. (2017). The Draft.

https://www.history.com/topics/us-government/conscription

Jessie Kindig, (2008). Vietnam War: Draft Resistance. University of Washington. https://depts.washington.edu/antiwar/vietnam_draft.shtml

ABOUT THE AUTHOR

Margret (Peg) Beck

Margaret (Peg) Beck is a nationally certified senior human resources professional, who brings over 25 years of business experience as a chief human resources officer in both the public and private sectors. She is founder and co-consultant with her husband of Creative Consulting Associates, LLC, an adjunct professor for over 15 years, and Certified Leadership Coach and published author. She is available for seminars and workshops, retreats and speaking engagements based on her book, *Life Lessons: A Passport for Personal and Professional Success* and many other topics coordinated to meet client's needs.

Unity of Sarasota is her spiritual home where she continues to receive personal and spiritual transformation and serves wherever she is led.

Her mission statement for her life is:

"Do whatever you can, whenever you can, to leave the world a better place."

THREE

Unexpected Change: A Catalyst for Spiritual Transformation

By Peg Beck

Now today…I have set before you, life and death, blessings, and curses. Now choose life…. —Deuteronomy 30:19

Many of us may be interested in, even excited by, change when we have created it. Buying and moving to a nicer home of our choosing, taking a trip to a new place, trying a new hobby or athletic pursuit---each may be very exciting. At one time in my career I was hired into a job as a "change agent". There was a new administration, new culture, and many new goals to pursue. I was in seventh heaven because I was one of the staff who was instigating and implementing the changes. Many of the other long-term employees were not so happy about the changes. I soon realized I had to include them in determining and implementing the changes, after a couple of significant failures. People are most inclined to accept change when they are included in developing and implementing the change.

What happens when an unexpected change occurs? A change in health, job loss, family issues or death – or perhaps a pandemic. How do we deal with that change? That is when we are forced to re-evaluate our thinking and consider how to manage the change.

The ending of my 30-year marriage was such a catalyst! I was almost 50 years old. My husband and I had raised three wonderful children to adulthood, and I expected that we would grow old together celebrating new family experiences. My spiritual beliefs, the teachings of my church, and the vows that I made were that marriage was for life. Then my husband said he no longer wanted to be married. He wanted to "do his own thing" and wanted a divorce. I cannot describe the shock that I felt. My world was spinning. It felt like a bad dream, although I knew it was real. It seemed to me that almost 30 years meant something to fight for. We had weathered many storms together. We should be able to get through this one, too. My stubbornness, denial, and need to be in control kept me from reality and moving on. Through two years of separation, tears, shock, counseling, Al-anon support groups, and help from friends, I was forced to evaluate my life and determine what *I* wanted. **I really had no idea!** When my counselor asked me that question, I could not give her an answer. My identity was as wife, mother, employee, supervisor.

What did I want now?

After two years, nothing had changed in my situation but me. I had moved to my own home, went out on a couple of dates, and learned about who I was as an individual.

It was then that I had a significant spiritual experience which became the catalyst for my spiritual transformation.

I was on a retreat and took some quiet time in the library at the conference site. The peace felt palatable to me. Books were often my refuge and where I found answers to so many of my questions. As I perused the books, I pulled out a Bible and opened it randomly, as I often did.

The Bible fell open to the Book of Deuteronomy, not one of my favorite books of the Bible. The words jumped off the page, and it was like I audibly heard the words:

Now today ...I have set before you. life and death, blessings, and curses. Now choose life....

The voice was as real as someone sitting beside me whispering in my ear. I knew in my heart that this was the guidance I had been seeking. I felt a peace that was indescribable. I knew it was time to make decisions and change my life.

A few days later was Valentine's Day. My husband came to my house and brought flowers to my adult daughter and me.

"Has anything changed? Are you ready to go to counseling?" I asked as we sat in the dining room alone.

"No," was his response. "Nothing has changed." Although somewhat deflated, I knew what I had to do.

"Then I want a divorce," the most difficult words that I never expected to say fell from my lips, although they came out more easily than I expected. Our lives were taking different paths and it was time for each of us to move on separately. An end to the life I had known! Although this was an end to the limbo I felt I was living in, the closure felt like a giant weight was lifted from my shoulders. I had no idea what my future meant.

The unknown! For me this was the most difficult place to be. I am a planner. I like to see the pathway ahead. But that is not how life takes us. Faith is the decision to move forward, even in the darkness and in spite of our fear.

A few months later our divorce was final. Soon after our youngest son was married, and we would be together again. While there was some sadness in me, we navigated the wedding smoothly and celebrated this beautiful family event together. The inner peace I felt in the guidance I received continued with me.

I did not know it then, but this was the beginning of one of the biggest spiritual transformations of my life. When I returned home, I went to my usual Al-anon meeting. After the meeting I spoke to a man – a new attendee - who had spoken at the meeting. I remembered how difficult those first few meetings were, so I went to encourage him. How amazing Spirit works!

Soon we started dating. This was the beginning of my most wonderful relationship with the man who would become my husband and my life partner of the past 25 years. He invited me to attend church with him and I agreed, although I had been an active member of another denomination. That first service in a New Thought church was like none I had ever experienced before. I heard the minister's talk like he was talking directly to me. I was hearing principles that I had believed for many years, but never heard taught anywhere else I had attended church.

"You are made in the image and likeness of God" … yes, I had heard that, but there was that God out there somewhere, not that I was one with this God. That life is a learning experience and we are "good, perfect and complete" just as we are – no more guilt - just learning experiences.

Each week I heard more uplifting positive talks that began to transform my life. This man and I were on a spiritual journey together with New Thought and the principles that changed our lives.

This was one of the most profound spiritually transforming experiences of my life. There have been others that continued to teach me that "Change" is often the catalyst to a transformation. Slowly I have learned that pain usually happens when I choose to stay in the experience that I know, rather than trying to move through an **unknown** that often becomes more satisfying.

Several years later another major change was thrust upon me. Although I was unhappy in my job, I had no intention of leaving until I had found another position. I had been the Vice President of Administration at a mental health facility and hospital at the time. While I was searching for a new job, the President called me to her office for an unscheduled meeting. As soon as I settled into my seat, she told me that my position was being eliminated due to budget cuts. That shock was another that I would not have invited into my life. Thankfully, my faith had grown some by then and in my better moments, I trusted that there was something better awaiting me. But, as the months of searching dragged on, the wheels of my mind began turning to change my thinking and remind myself that God only wanted good for me and it just was not visible yet.

After five months of searching, I was invited for an interview in another town at a mental health facility as its human resources director. My husband and I knew it would mean a move and we began investigating housing while we were there. After my interview it appeared that I had the position, when the manager told me I was "the top candidate."

When I received the news that I was not selected, I was devastated...again. However, the more we thought about it, my husband and I realized that this was a gift--we really did not want to move. We decided I would continue to search in our own local area.

A day or two after we made that decision, I saw an ad in a local paper that I had not seen before. I applied, and a few days later I was called for an interview. After an extensive interviewing process, I was offered and accepted the position as Director of Human Resources at the local college in my hometown! I discovered later that it had been open for some time and that there were 125 other applicants that had been considered. Perhaps that open position was waiting for me.

I soon learned that academia was a much better fit for me. I loved the atmosphere of being in a learning environment working with others who enjoyed learning as much as I did. I retired from that college 16 years later and continue to work there as a part time adjunct faculty member. Soon after I started my own consulting business, began writing chapters in books to help empower other women, and recently completed my first book: *Life Lessons: A passport for personal and professional success.*

What have I learned from these experiences?

1. Change is inevitable. Learning to deal with change is necessary for my survival.

2. Unexpected change may force me to change the way I view my life and the world– it often becomes the catalyst for a spiritual transformation. For me, **fear** is the emotion that initially sets in when an unexpected change appears. I become disoriented and often feel incompetent to adjust to the change. At first, I resist the change and argue for all the reasons why this change will not work or is not necessary.

3. The sooner I move to faith and trust that "Letting go and letting God" is the best way to live my life the sooner I will find the guidance to navigate the situation. When I let go of controlling the things I cannot change, I am more at peace. My faith has grown through each of the major changes in my life and I soon remember that God has been with me through every big change and has brought more gifts into my life that I would have missed without the change.

4. Change drives transformation. Through transformation, our lives and experiences may become richer. Many inventions have made our lives easier than those before us. Some may not appreciate the changes, for example the loss of farming and rural life from the industrial revolution or meeting virtually, rather than in person. Others gain work and new opportunities from the same change.

Currently, we are all living with the unexpected changes caused by the pandemic. So many have suffered through illness, death of family members and friends, loss of jobs and businesses. **How can we think that any good is coming from this change?**

    We have been able to stay connected virtually, that previously were not options, which has been the new way of keeping our relationships and social contacts. These technological products spawned by someone's creative idea have spread quickly throughout our lives. Here are just a few of the virtual gifts that I have experienced and that you might relate to:

- We celebrated my sister's 65th birthday celebration and daughter-in-law's 40th birthday with family and friends from 100's of miles away. Many who would not have been able to celebrate with us in person attended. Some, I had never met.

- Learning to teach on-line college classes. Something I have avoided for over 15 years!

- A few days ago, I "virtually" attended the funeral of a friend's husband, along with people from all over the country. While not the ideal that families would have liked, it provided a way that we could mourn together.

- Our church services, small group meetings, and even my Chair Yoga class are available to me through Zoom technology.

- I continue to conduct my consulting business virtually when I used to travel to the client site to accomplish these projects.

    That is not to say that I do not miss the personal contact of others. I do. But transformation and change are the ways creation continues to evolve.

Before the pandemic only 4% of employees worked from home. Currently, 37% of jobs are being conducted from home and over 80% of workers state they would like to work from home at least part time. Employers are considering why they need to spend so much on brick and mortar buildings and will soon make remote work part of their plan – saving millions of dollars for employers and employees in reduced travel.

I am sure that we will experience more major transformations than we ever dreamed of and new businesses will begin from other creative ideas. Others go out of business if they do not change.

But how do we navigate those difficult transitional times of change? We can go through them kicking and screaming, wondering "why is this happening to me?" or we can learn to trust Spirit and move through the process of change in a positive way and maybe eventually even enjoy the ride.

Butterflies provide an excellent example of experiencing huge change, called metamorphosis, although it happens by natural instinct. Butterflies often symbolize life's transformation. Without the metamorphosis of the caterpillar we would never experience the beauty of butterflies. I use the symbol of a butterfly as a reminder to me of the potential for growth and beauty that major changes may make in my life.

In my book, *Life Lessons: A Passport for Personal and Professional Success*, I used this description of navigating the change process from Martha Beck in her book *Growing Wings: The Power of Change*, as she discusses the *Phases of Human Metamorphosis*.

We go through these phases, more or less in order, after any major change catalyst (death of a loved one, falling in love or breaking up, getting or losing a job, having children or emptying the nest, or navigating through the changes brought on by this pandemic.)

The strategies for dealing with change depend on the magnitude of the change you are experiencing some are more difficult than others. Briefly the phases are as follows:

Phase 1: Dissolving (Similar to the Denial stage of grief.)
We feel like we have lost our identity and are left temporarily formless. We may feel that everything is falling apart. Depending on the change, we may feel like we are losing everyone and everything. It may feel like death because it is the demise of the person you have been.

What are some tools we can use?.

- *Live One Day (or 10 minutes or 10 seconds) at a Time*

- *"Cocoon" by Caring for Yourself in Physical, Immediate Ways*
  Do what it takes to comfort yourself.

- *Talk to Others Who Have Gone Through a Metamorphosis*
  Allow yourself to share your feelings and listen to someone else who has transformed through a similar experience

- *Let Yourself Grieve* We will go through the normal grief process of loss - denial, anger, sadness, (even depression) and acceptance many times. The more we allow ourselves to experience these feelings, the sooner we can feel our transformation. One of my favorite books that helped me through these stages of grief is *"How to Survive the Loss of a Love"* by Dr. Harold H. Bloomfield, M.D., Melbe Colgrove, Ph.D., & Peter McWilliams. The over-riding premise is "It is hard to look back on any gain in life that does not have a loss attached to it. With this firmly in mind we can examine the various losses in life."

> *Make a gratitude list.* There is always something to be grateful for. It may start with "I woke up this morning!" or "I can breathe, or walk, or talk…" The more you begin to put everyday things on the list that you take for granted, the more easily you will begin to move into Phase 2.

Phase 2: Imagining

Phase 2 is a welcome phase because we begin to feel we have some control. Using prayer or mediation, walking in the woods or on the beach, listening to music, or however we get our peaceful connection with the Divine helps us to find creative ways to move through our transformation.

Like the first phase, you cannot speed up the process any more than a butterfly can speed up the process from cocoon to flying out. The maple tree cannot resist the winter if it is to produce its wonderful maple syrup.

Let Yourself Daydream

Create imaginary scenarios, even if they feel impossible at the moment. Just give yourself time to sit, think dream. Write down your dreams and your ideas to make them a reality. You are moving into Phase 3.

Phase 3: Re-forming

Now the implementation stage is the phase I like because I am about taking action. For those of us who thrive on "getting it done," this is a wonderful phase. Make a start—walk through the fear. Re-forming your life, like anything new, complex, and important, inevitably brings up problems you did not expect.

- *Be Willing to Start Over* Every time your new plan fails, and you briefly go back to Phase 1, feeling disoriented, remind yourself of Thomas Edison's famous quote, "I have not failed. I've just found 10,000 ways that won't work." Repeat it as a mantra if necessary. Keep de-bugging and re-implementing until your plan works, which it eventually will! Now is the time you are ready to move to Phase 4.

Phase 4: Flying – Becoming a butterfly!

- *Enjoy!* Allow yourself to bask in your new reality. Applaud yourself! Treat yourself to something that you may consider an extravagance –whatever **healthy** indulgence you can give to yourself.

- *Make a gratitude list* – AGAIN! Make another list---see how much it has changed from your list when you were going through Phase 1. Remember faith has brought you through to a new beginning.

In knowing how to deal with metamorphosis, whenever it occurs, remember these tools. These four phases are the process of Change!

"Change your thinking, change your life!"

It has transformed me and brought me to a peace beyond understanding. Now it's your turn.

Thoughts to Ponder

1. What unanticipated change has shown up in my life that was a Catalyst for Personal Transformation for me?

2. Which of these phases did I experience and how did these phases feel?

3. What tools did I use to help me through these stages?

4. Describe how you were transformed at the end, and what you learned from it?

Affirmation – *I know that I am whole and perfect today and can choose to be a different kind of perfect tomorrow.*

References:

The Thompson Chain-Reference Bible, New International Version, 1983,

The B.B. Kirkbride Bible Company, Inc., Indianapolis, Indiana and Zondervan Corporation, Grand Rapids, Michigan.

Five Stages of Grief: On Death and Dying

Elizabeth Kubler-Ross, 1969, Scribner, NY, NY

Growing Wings: the Power of Change

https://marthabeck.com/2003/01/growing-wings-the-power-of-change/

How to Survive the Loss of a Love, by Dr. Harold H. Bloomfield, M.D., Melbe Colgrove, Ph.D., & Peter McWilliams, 1976, Leo Press, Inc., Allen Park, Michigan

Life Lessons: A Passport for Personal and Professional Success

Peg Beck, 2018, Peg Beck, Sarasota, FL

Notes:

ABOUT THE AUTHOR

Rev. Dr. Suzi Schadle

Rev. Dr. Suzi Schadle is Senior Minister at Unity of Sarasota, A Beacon of Light and Love: Opening Minds, Touching Hearts, Transforming Lives. She's a gifted speaker and facilitator. Before ministry, Suzi was a successful corporate executive. She blends her diverse skills to inspire people to: Awaken to their Passion, Discover their Purpose, Activate the Path that Unfolds it, and Live as the Promise of its Fulfillment. Suzi was born in Germany and adopted by an American family. She studied music at Peabody Conservatory in Baltimore while in high school. Suzi still plays soprano, alto, and bass silver flutes with joy and passion.

FOUR

The Day I Stopped Being A Fool

By Rev. Dr. Suzi Schadle

March 31, 1982 had been pretty routine; I had worked a long day as Food and Beverage Manager at the Seattle Downtown Hilton. After I had closed up the lobby bar at midnight, I headed over to the Mayflower Hotel where a good friend was tending bar. It had become my end-of day habit to enjoy "free drinks" for generous tips until 2 AM closing, or more often, after hours—a perk of being in the hospitality business.

This current modus operandi had started after my mother died suddenly ten months prior. Before that I had abstained from booze for three years, not because I thought it was a good idea; but to prove to friends who said I had a drinking problem that they were wrong, and that I could stop at any time. I didn't change any thoughts or feelings; I just stopped drinking. I was like an angry raw nerve the whole time. I'm sure some people would have paid me to drink again in hopes I'd be less of a volatile jerk.

This particular April Fools' eve, I was up for a big night of drinking. When my bartender friend ended the party at 3 AM, one of the other after-hours drinkers suggested heading to a nearby bar for after-after-hours. I was very drunk by then and don't recall much about the place. Around 4 AM, someone I didn't even know suggested we continue the party at his house in West Seattle. I jumped at the idea, got in my car, and started on the 30-minute drive to the after-after-after party. A few miles down the road on Interstate 5, I had just a moment of lucidity. "What am I thinking! It's 4:00 in the morning and I have to be at work at 5! You fool, you fool, you fool!" I pulled onto the shoulder, turned off the car, leaned my head on the steering wheel, and promptly passed out.

I was startled awake by someone knocking on the driver-side window and then a bright light in my face. Then I noticed the flashing blue light, and an officer motioned for me to roll down the window. "Have you been drinking this evening?" "Yes, sir I have." "How much?" "A lot, I've been drinking a lot. Guilty, I'm very drunk." "Well, I'm afraid you're going to have to go to the station for a breathalyzer. We'll have your car towed there." After I failed the test miserably, they charged me and let me go. I walked up to the Hilton and told another Manager friend I wouldn't be at work, and since she was just getting off shift, she drove me home.

April Fools' Day 1982 was both the most foolish day of my life and the day I stopped being a fool. I had been taken into Police Headquarters in downtown Seattle, given a breathalyzer test, and charged with "physical control." Even though I wasn't caught driving my car while intoxicated, I was in "physical control" of it: behind the wheel, keys in the ignition, and parked on the shoulder of I-5.

After I was released from police custody, and my friend drove me home; my life changed forever. As I lay on my bed watching my chest rise and fall as I breathed, I thought: "God, please just let the breath go out of me and never come back in again." It wasn't that I wanted to kill myself; I just didn't want to live anymore.

Suddenly, I heard a voice. It was odd though; it was audible in my ears; and, at the same time it was in my head. I sat straight up and looked around the room to see who was there. The voice said: "It is not your time to die. I have things for you to do." Something inside me knew it was the voice of God. April Fools' Day 1982 was the lowest point in my life, and it was also the springboard of a life-long and profound awakening for me.

I called a friend who had been concerned about my drinking and asked her if she would take me to an AA meeting that night. She enthusiastically agreed and asked if I wanted to search out a meeting or if she should find one. I told her I knew the one I wanted to go to; it was one where I could face another part of myself that I had been in denial about—I needed to go to a gay AA meeting. She didn't seem surprised. As we drove up to the meeting place, I noticed a co-worker walking in. "Oh no, I work with that guy!" "You want to wait and go to a different meeting?" "No, I've come this far, I need to walk through that door. I've let people see me at my worst, what could be the harm in letting people see me cleaning up my act?"

I sat nervously through the meeting, listening, not saying a word. At the end of the meeting Dale, my co-worker, made a beeline for me. "Your expression says you think I'm gonna send out a memo at work telling everyone where I saw you. Remember, I'm here for the same reason you are, and this *is* Alcoholics Anonymous. I'm sure you don't remember, but I ran into you late last night and prayed that one day you'd find this place; I never dreamed it'd happen so soon. I'm glad you're here, and I am here for you and there for you at work too."

Later that week I met with a lawyer who specialized in drunk driving cases. "So, you want to try and beat this thing?" "No, I don't, because I'm guilty and I want to get help before I manage to kill myself or someone else. I've been to AA meetings every day since this happened and I've signed up for out-patient treatment. I want you to help me hang onto my driver's license and avoid being forced to go to 30-day in-patient treatment; otherwise, I may lose my job." "Wow, this is refreshing; most of my clients just want me to beat the charges. I'll petition the court for a deferred prosecution. If accepted, you'll be on probation for three years; during which time, you go to some sort of treatment, go to AA regularly, see a parole officer once a month, and have no further incidents. If you do all that, then in three years the whole thing is erased from your record. Good luck, you know, I think you just might make it."

I started my out-patient treatment, went to AA every night, I met with my parole officer, who I really seemed to click with. I was on my way to recovery and getting my life back. A friend told me about this positive church that I might like, so I decided to give it a try. As soon as the music started the energy felt great. Then Rev. Jim spoke, and I knew I was home!

I had been a spiritual seeker ever since I was a small child, I studied various religions in college and tried out several, but no one faith seemed to resonate for me. I had come to the conclusion that I was going to have to create my own sort of spirituality that drew from the essence of various spiritual traditions. Somewhere along the way, I had lost my way, and had lost my motivation to create that personal spirituality. That Sunday at Seattle Church of Religious Science I realized that someone, Rev. Dr. Ernest Holmes, had already synthesized and woven the essence of many spiritual traditions into this wonderful philosophy, faith, and way of life. And lots of other people resonated with it too. I was home; I had found my tribe! As I walked down the aisle to leave, I looked over and noticed Don, my parole officer. I nodded and he said: "It's so good to see you here." We chatted briefly, and I learned that he was actually a Licensed Prayer Practitioner at the church. I felt divinely guided and blessed.

A whole new world was opening for me, and my life was beginning to make sense and come together both inside and out. At work, I had gotten an amazing career opportunity to move out of Food and Beverage management and into Sales and Marketing. I was continuing with all my commitments to staying clean and sober, and I felt better than I had in years. I was committed to church and started taking classes there.

One night in class, Rev. Jim led us through a guided meditation and then asked us to write our uncensored obituary in our journal. It was challenging because what I was writing came fast and clear, but I couldn't imagine it was actually about me. It was all about me becoming a powerful Religious Science Minister and all the lives I had touched throughout my ministry. I was a bit freaked out; I couldn't imagine that God was calling me! Then I remembered that as a young Catholic kid, God was my best friend, like my friends' imaginary playmates, only not imaginary. As a kid I had wanted to be a priest, even in the face of my brothers telling me girls couldn't even be altar boys! I wore a robe and played priest with friends, having them kneel in front of me as I gave them Necco Wafers for communion. It was good to retrieve those childhood dreams.

But grown-up Suzi couldn't quite embrace it, so "I put aside childish things" along with my journal from class and didn't think or speak of it again. What made sense to me now was that my corporate career was taking off like a moonshot, and I could see me being successful in that arena. I fulfilled my deferred prosecution with congratulations from the judge, my lawyer, my parole officer, and the policeman who arrested me. They touted me as a poster child for rehabilitation. Life was good! I was soon hired as Director of Sales and Marketing for Hotel Pontchartrain in Detroit. While it was a bumpy ride with the unethical and illegal actions of the owner, Charles Keating, of the infamous Savings and Loan scandal of the 1980's; I was able to parlay my own success there into a huge leap in my career. Yes, cleaning up the wreckage of my past and resurrecting my spiritual life was paying off.

I was hired as Vice President of Sales and Marketing for North America by a Swedish company, Sara Hotels. I was based in New York City with an office in Dallas as well, where I was President of our subsidiary hotel chain, Park Suites. I traveled to Scandinavia and around the U.S. constantly. I had made it; this was the life: big salary, lots of perks; and boy did I look important. I worked hard and I was successful not only for myself, but for the company as well.

I had reached the top of the corporate ladder; I was the highest-ranking woman in the company world-wide and I was only 35 years old! "Wow, look at me; but don't look into me."

There was a flaw in this happy picture; there was a chink in my armor. I began to realize I was a workaholic, obsessed with and consumed by this quest for success. What was I trying to prove? Who was I trying to be? My work had become my life; my position had become my identity. I looked the picture of success, but inside I felt empty—spiritually bankrupt. I didn't have time for my 12-Step meetings and church anymore; and now, I felt as miserable as I had right before I hit bottom and got sober. This time, the drug I was using was work and the carefully crafted persona that I presented to the world. It certainly insulated me from myself. And it protected me from other people; after all, if I never let anyone know the real me, they wouldn't be able to hurt the real me. The problem is, if you lock people out, you lock yourself in. I had lost myself again and I wasn't even drinking. "You fool, you fool, you fool!" I had taken back my fool's mantle… it was merely an updated style.

I was devastated at the realization, but I had been here before and I knew to seek help. By this time, I had been charged with moving our Dallas corporate office to Orlando, Florida. So, it was there that I found Choices Counseling and joined a therapy group. I hated group therapy when I first started. I sensed that this was going to push me to dig deep; and I wouldn't be able to play intellectual dodge ball like I had been able to do with one-on-one counseling in the past. I was right, the therapy was intense; and it got me to a point I knew I was confronting my deepest most hidden core issues.

It was a surprising glimpse into my true self and an unmasking of the persona I had created as a child that I didn't realize wasn't real. My "story" was so well-produced and cemented that the very thought of unpacking and discarding it was terrifying. I literally feared that if I let go of the person I had made up, a "real" Suzi might not actually exist. My head knew that was silly, but my heart was in panic mode. I decided to buckle down, or more accurately, let go of my BS and do my inner work. At times it felt like an earthmover machine was excavating my innards! Soon the pain began to give way to relief and peace as I released what was not me and began to rediscover who I truly was. I returned to my 12-Step meetings and church for additional support; amazingly I managed to make the time in my busy important life.

As I resurrected my spiritual life, I retrieved the fragmented and scattered pieces of myself and I began to feel whole. I felt joy in my journey as I made friends with myself and realized I actually liked this person. The healthier I became mentally, emotionally, and spiritually the less I was able to comfortably play the role I had crafted in my work life. The two were incompatible.

I called for a meeting with my boss, and very calmly told him: "I don't want to do this anymore; I'm not happy and I've given up too much of me and my life for something that doesn't bring me joy and doesn't really make the world a better place."

Nils had replaced my original boss, Hans, and we hadn't hit it off well at all. So, his response amazed me: "I think this is a wonderful understanding to have for yourself and I congratulate you on your honesty and courage. You deserve a life you enjoy. I wish you all the best." I offered to stay until they could find someone to replace me, but Nils said: "No, you've given enough, you deserve to start your new life now. I'm going to give your three months of severance pay with your benefits. Feel free to use your car, your office, and your secretary until you've made other arrangements. We appreciate all you've done here for us."

I ended up starting my own Leadership and Team Building consulting firm; and, thanks to Nils, Sara Hotels was my first client. There was a dramatic shift being an "outside expert" rather than an employee. They actually listened to my more progressive ideas about the importance of focusing on the people component of the business and not just the bottom line. We did some wonderful and rewarding work together.

It's amazing how powerfully and easily life unfolds when you live from your authenticity; the universe conspires in support. After a few consulting gigs, it dawned on me that I didn't need to stay in Orlando. I moved back to my beloved Seattle and put out my consulting shingle there. I bought a beautiful condo right on Lake Union at the south end of downtown with a view of the Space Needle and mountains and gorgeous sunsets. I was able to reconnect with old friends and colleagues. My consulting business was doing well and yet afforded me time to focus on my spiritual life. I got to re-engage with my original New Thought church. I still knew lots of people; but there was a new minister, Rev. Kathianne. She was a dynamic speaker, charismatic from the pulpit. This was exciting. I could see myself getting deeply involved; I volunteered, joined the music program and started taking classes again. I felt this would be the centerpiece of my new life. Interestingly, I celebrated my fortieth birthday upon my return to Seattle; my midlife crisis turned out to be my midlife opportunity for awakening.

A class I took shortly after my return provided me with one of the most powerful wake-up calls of my life. The Assistant Minister, Rev. Janet, led us through a guided meditation and then asked us to write our uncensored obituary in our journal. This seemed familiar. I started writing all about me becoming a powerful Religious Science Minister and all the lives I had touched throughout my ministry. I was a bit freaked out; I was having a vivid déjà vu experience! Then a light bulb exploded in my head; this was not déjà vu. This was real; I had actually done this exact exercise before with the same experience. I raced home after class and dug through a box I hadn't unpacked yet and found my journal from the class I had taken with Rev. Jim years ago. I flipped through and found my previous obituary; it was almost verbatim with the one I had just written. Then I looked at the date; it was exactly ten years prior, to the day!

I knew this time it was the voice of Spirit calling me to ministry. God hadn't made a mistake tapping me years ago; I just wasn't ready to embrace who I had come here to be. Spirit had never really let me go all those years, but simply waited patiently for me to wake up and say: "Yes!" This new revelation remained between God and me for the time being. I finished all my foundational classes, began Licensed Prayer Practitioner classes, and enrolled in the Ministerial classes open to non-ministerial students—I took them for credit just in case I really committed.

At the very next Ministerial graduation ceremony, I was moved to tears and so inspired that I calmly turned to my friend Lisa and said: "I'm going to be a minister." "Are you just figuring that out? Everybody knows that about you!"

The next day I officially enrolled in Ministerial School. One day, in my senior year, I was doing my morning meditation as usual, but it was anything but usual. In my mind's eye I kept seeing what looked like puzzle pieces floating down into the lid of a box. I thought it strange imagery for me because I always hated puzzles. Impatiently, I was always tempted the cut pieces to fit and cram them into the puzzle and be done with it. This was different; I just let the pieces fall without the urge to get it done. For the next several weeks the same thing happened in my meditations. One day, the pieces began to fit themselves together and the picture was clear, not so much as a picture, but as a feeling with explicit detail. I was called to start a church on the eastside of Lake Washington; and open on November 7, 1999! I had never even considered starting a church; and yet, this was clearly my call.

Within days of this revelation, people started calling me, saying they heard I was starting a church and wanted to be part of it. Since I hadn't shared this vision with anyone, I asked how they had heard, and not one of them had an answer. I graduated in June 1999, passed my written licensing exams and oral panels, and received my Ministerial License in October 1999. I began searching for a place for our new church at a time it was almost impossible to rent anything even at exorbitant prices. I didn't want to be in a strip mall or a hotel; but out of desperation I went to the Redmond Inn to talk to the Catering Director. I told her I wanted to rent space for church services; she asked what denomination. I had dreaded that question, as our teaching was often considered a whacky woo-woo cult, but I held my breath and told her. She gushed with enthusiasm: "I go to Unity, and I love Center for Spiritual Living!" She gave us the deal of the century and we opened Center for Spiritual Living Eastside in Redmond, a suburb of Seattle, November 7, 1999 to an attendance of 99 people. We were on our way. I felt I was in my rightful place, in alignment with Spirit, and comfortable in my own skin.

A year later, I opened a Ministerial Campus; and in the next ten years we celebrated over twenty graduates who are now leading powerful ministries of their own. During my eleven years serving Center for Spiritual Living Eastside we moved the church ten times, touching even more lives than if we'd stayed in one place. I got another vividly clear call from God to step away from my church and start an online ministry, and to also facilitate church leadership development for other churches. I later led several interim ministries helping churches vision and attract the right minister for them. In March 2018 I became Senior Minister at Unity of Sarasota where I remain to this day. While my ministry has morphed over twenty years, Spirit's call is the same: to remember who I have come here to be, and to love and serve from that remembrance.

My journey is to go within: I find God, I find myself. Sometimes we must "go in, to find out." When we shift our focus from outside-in to inside-out, Spirit conspires for our good.

April Fools' Day 1982 I stopped being a fool. Today, I am a fool for God, and I wouldn't have it any other way! Blessings on Your Journey of Awakening and Transformation....

Notes:

ABOUT THE AUTHOR

Betty Mann McQueen

Betty Mann McQueen uses her life experiences as teaching opportunities for herself and others. Her ability to fast forward through the drama of circumstances with optimism shines through her writing and programs which are practical and inspirational. Betty's life reflects a journey of love in action. She uses examples of how to move forward for a life of joy and fulfilled dreams by using Universal Principles as embodied in the Unity Movement. She presented her first workshop two weeks after being interviewed at the Unity Church of Sarasota, Florida, before becoming an active member June 12, 1988.

Updates to
Pathways of Spiritual Awakening:
Uplifting Stories of Personal Transformation

Thank you for purchasing your copy of Pathways of Spiritual Awakening: Uplifting Stories of Personal Transformation.

The Editorial Board wishes to apologize for the following oversights in the editing of this book.

Delete

Pg. 105 Line 29
"A blank
Pg. 106 Line 1
"copy of the one-page worksheet is at the end of the story."
Pg. 109 Line 17 & 18
"On the next page is Bryon Katie's worksheet that she has students complete prior to every one of her classes".

Add

Pg. 109 Line 16
A link is provided for those who wish to view this form.
https://thework.com/wp-content/uploads/2019/07/jyn_en_mod_6feb2019_r4_form1.pdf

Change

Pg. 136 Line 26 Spacing
...their 14-room.....

Blessing on Your Journey
Unity of Sarasota Editorial Board

FIVE

It's All About Perspective

By Betty Mann McQueen

"I never lose. I either win or learn."
These are the words that put life in perspective
When we know they are the words
Of Nelson Mandela!

How can I complain about
A government mandated lockdown
From my comfortable home
Surrounded by my treasures,
Including the technology
To connect with the outside world,
When a man imprisoned
In isolation for 27 years
Under deplorable conditions can say,
"I never lose. I either win or learn."

*Yes, that puts **my** life in perspective!*

His powerful words are my new mantra,
My three-second reminder
To act mindfully
Rather than to react to situations
Perpetuated by the COVID-19 virus
Which has permeated the fabric of our world,
Creating a pandemic with a domino effect
Changing the world and each one of us.

For the first time in my memory
The healthy are being quarantined,
Thus changing family dynamics.
Businesses either closed,
Sending workers home without pay,
Or made electronic provisions
For employees to work from home.

Parents not only have to adjust
To a different work environment
Or a loss of income
But, in essence, are mandated
To homeschool their children,
Causing a wider chasm between
The haves and the have nots
As virtual communication
Becomes the norm for those
Who can afford the technology.

*I choose to **not** own a TV, but I still see*
And I still experience more anger
Than before the pandemic,
Anger triggered by fear,
Economic uncertainty, misconceptions,
Forced lifestyle changes,
And negativity reinforced by the media.

*I choose to **not** be caught up in that world.*
I choose to act with wisdom and compassion.
But it's not easy in the pandemic world.
Sometimes situations upset my inner peace
And I do react rather than act
With wisdom and compassion.

There are times when three seconds
Are all I have to diffuse anger—
Either mine or another's—
And to create a positive experience.
Hurtful words, once spoken,
Cannot be unsaid.

By using my three-second mantra
Inspired by Nelson Mandela,
I can tap into the all-powerful
All-knowing, Universal God-mind.
Using that wisdom available to all,
I never lose. I win. I learn.
And so does everyone involved.

I live alone.
So in addition to my three-second mantra,
What do I have going for me
To prevent the mandated social distancing
From crossing that fine line
Into social isolation?

Several weeks into the lockdown,
A friend called, asking,
"How are you doing?"
Without hesitation, I replied,
"God and I are doing fine. We talk a lot."

Himself, a man of faith,
Was slow to respond
As we both thought about
The differences in our situations.
He and I married the same year.
He and his wife of 52 years are self-isolating.
I've been widowed for 8 of those 52 years.
Although we both have the God-connection,
He has the daily human connection. I don't.

He asked, "Are you lonely?"

"No. I sometimes feel alone.
But lonely? No."

He asked, "Why do you think that is?"
I surprised myself with my answer.
"Because I like myself."

Reflecting on our conversation later,
I realized, if I do feel lonely,
It's when I'm with people.
Lonely is that lost feeling
When I'm with people I know
And I am again that teenager
Hanging on the fringes,
Not understanding the inside jokes.
It's that feeling of being invisible in a crowd.

But I'm no longer a teenager.
I'm into my ninth decade
And I've learned some social skills,
Plus, I like the woman I've become.

Now I push past that feeling
Of isolation in a crowd by
Finding the person who looks
More uncomfortable than I feel,
Introduce myself,
Ask a leading question,
And mindfully listen more than talk.
I never lose. I win because
I have a new best friend in the making!

How does this practice translate
From pre-pandemic to living the pandemic?
The pandemic limits my in-person contacts.
So I write more letters and emails.
I make more phone calls. Send more texts.
I pray more prayers of gratitude
Which are my reminders
To write more thank you notes.

I take more time to count my blessings.
Topping my list of blessings
Is my relationship with God.
Although God isn't a person,
We have a personal relationship.
God permeates all I AM—all I do.

God is the Spirit, the Light within me.
God is all around me.
God is why I like myself.
The Christ consciousness,
The divinity of God, is within me.
How can I not like and love myself
If my very essence is of God?

I see myself as a co-creator with God,
Hence, as a positive thinking person,
I can weather a pandemic.
I never lose. I win. I learn. I thrive.
God is my constant in a changing world,

Pandemic or no pandemic.

Second on my gratitude list
Is an appreciation for God's gift
Of all the resources I need,
One being a monthly social security check.
A regular income is a privilege
Not everyone can experience.
Mine is not a sustainable income,
And I admit, there are times
I momentarily forget the promises of God
And I allow fear to cloud my faith.

But eventually, love pushes out the fear
As both cannot live in the same space,
And I experience God's abundance
Through the generosity of gifts
Of cash, checks, goods, and services
From toilet paper and food
To repairs on my 1925 vintage home.

The Law of Attraction at work.
I have enough to spare and to share.
Thus the cycle of giving and receiving
Continues to flow during the pandemic
Because my experiment in tithing
Is an established, on-going practice.
Also, I'm given opportunities to earn
Additional income in keeping

*With my calling, my purpose, my mission.
I'm deeply appreciative.
I never lose. I win. I thrive.*

*I realize that, for many,
Social distancing in a home
Is not a privilege
Everyone can experience.
For some, homes are small
And some homes must house
Extended family under one roof.
And many families are not experienced
In sharing their space twenty-four seven.*

*From this perspective,
I'm deeply appreciative for my home,
A twelve hundred square-foot space
Planned for two, hence spacious for one.
It is my sanctuary, my retreat, my quiet place.*

*I wish whoever coined social distancing
Would have put more thought into it.
Physical distancing is more appropriate.
We are social beings and human connections
Keep us healthy in body, mind, and spirit.*

*Yes, masks hide smiles,
But they don't hide smiling eyes.
The mandated six-feet physical distancing*

Doesn't prevent social conversation—
Even speaking through a mask!
I am amazed how startled people are
When I start a conversation.
But I'm not surprised when they
Enthusiastically continue the dialogue.

My once-a-week trip to Walmart
Is often my salvation from sliding
Into the pit of social isolation,
At the bottom of the pit is depression.
A place I don't want to be!

Phone conversations, zoom meetings, texts,
Emails, and all forms of social media help.
But for me?
They do not give me that human connection
I need to feel part of the real world.
But either way, I never lose. I win. I learn.
I count my blessings.

And yes, I do venture into the world,
Mindfully practicing and honoring
Space and preferences of others with
Physical distancing, wearing masks,
Sanitizing often, and wearing gloves
In potentially compromising situations.

Washing hands, sanitizing, wearing gloves
Are not new ways of life for me—
In fact, months into the pandemic
I have yet to buy any gloves
As thus far, I still have an adequate supply.
They are a tool of my profession,
Family and consumer sciences,
Or for those of you who graduated
From high school before 1995,
Home economics.

A sense of humor is a saving grace,
And the fun days are the days
I wear the pink gloves and
My dress with the pink flowers.
It does my 82-year old heart good
When the young men, (Yes, the **young** *men,)*
Compliment me on my coordinated ensemble!

When cooking at home
Even before the pandemic,
I did wear gloves when handling
Food for large groups,
Especially for covered dish dinners.
Afterall, I've taught more than one class
On sanitation and food safety practices.

I can thank my sixty years as a
Family and consumer sciences

*Professional for opportunities in
Practicing, polishing, and updating
My essential life skills,
Basic competencies first introduced
By my parents and expanded
By high school and college
Home economics classes during
The first 22 years of my life.*

*What I've learned in dealing
With a crisis over the years is that,
Because I have the essential life skills,
I can act with wisdom and compassion
Regardless of the circumstances.
Thanks to family and consumer sciences,
I learn. I win. I learn. I grow
Even in this COVID-19 virus pandemic.*

*Because of family and consumer sciences,
I move from cope to manage and,
On many levels to master,
Thus giving me the resiliency necessary
When life gives me more thorns than roses.
I win. I thrive with inner and outer peace
Because I routinely practice a healthy lifestyle
With wellness as my goal.*

*It's a lifestyle which allows me
To adapt to conditions outside my control,*

Such as this pandemic.
I don't have the additional stress
Of learning how to meet my basic needs
Of food, clothing, and shelter.
I don't have to learn the basics skills,
Such as how to wash my hands.
That's lesson number one in any
Child development, parenting, or
Foods and nutrition class.
My drama in a crisis is shorter than many
In that I only have to deal with the issue
Because I already have my essential life skills.

Thanks to my divine calling,
Family and consumer sciences,
I can turn my focus to my divine purpose,
Which is teaching,
And to my divine mission which is
To empower others to fulfill
Their divine missions,
By supporting and teaching them
How to successfully navigate
Through new, uncomfortable,
Or traumatic experiences
Such as a pandemic, without panic.

I am one of the fortunate ones
In that, just like I don't remember a time
That I didn't know God,

I cannot remember a time
When I didn't know my divine purpose.
According to the family story, I was 5 when
I dramatically announced,
"Daddy, Daddy, I'm going to be a teacher
When I grow up!"

So at 5, I knew the "what"
And at 16, God showed the "how"
When I heard a college dean say,
"Home economics is not a subject.
It is an applied discipline.
If you become a home economics teacher,
You will teach anything and everything
Which relates to the family."

With that aha moment,
My purpose, my calling, my mission
Became a unified whole.
I was given permission
To teach a person—not a subject!
I embraced the concept of wholeness!

At 16, I didn't realize how all-encompassing
That would be until, as a newly minted teacher,
I included spiritual development,
Within my home economics curriculum,
Walking a very careful line through the years
Between separation of church and state

To create an environment of safety for students
To expose, but not impose, beliefs and values.

A friend well versed in comparative religions
Pointed out to me over 30 years ago,
My belief system is Unity.
She was right. It is.
My calling, my purpose, my mission
Have never changed.
Unity has helped me refine
The wording of my divine mission
As well as to dig deep to clarify and expand
My core beliefs and spiritual practices
So I can walk my talk regardless
Of the circumstances of my life—
Including the COVID-19 pandemic—
No matter how long it lasts.

I believe in a God of absolute good.
I don't believe God causes bad stuff.
You will never hear me say,
"I'm happy for the bad experiences."
What you'll hear me say is,
"This happened to me.
What can I learn from it?"
Paraphrasing Nelson Mandela,
I never lose. I win. I learn.
Because if I learn, I win.
I'm convinced it is possible to learn

From a good experience as from a bad one.

That includes spending more time alone
Without feeling lonely.
Which is quite an achievement for me,
Because upon reflection,
I've lived most of my life with someone.
Having parents with open hearts and an open door
To anyone who needed a temporary home,
My brother and I remember little of our early life
With only four people under our roof.
I lived "on my own" a little over 4 years
Before I married at 30.
My father, mother, and brother died before
I was widowed after 45 years of marriage.

And here I thought my not being lonely
Was because I had practice and experience
As an independent woman living alone!
But that wasn't the scenario.
I learned to be an independent woman
Because the people I lived with,
Including my husband,
Gave me opportunities to be independent.

I don't have children.
I do have relatives,
Both by birth and marriage.
But they don't live in my town,

So I make my own life,
With my family of choice—my friends.

Bottom line?
Alone is just a fact of my life,
Pandemic or no pandemic.
I live alone in my space.
Lonely is different.
Lonely is not my Truth,
Lonely means something is lacking.
Nothing is lacking in my life.

My circumstances are ever-changing,
Hence my life is never boring.
"They" say—whoever they are—
That we will meet 10,000 people in a lifetime.
To me that means there's always
Someone, somewhere, someplace
Who will extend an invitation to me
If I don't extend it first.
Sitting on the pity pot until I feel
Lonely or depressed is not an option!

I have a divine mission to complete
And it can only be done in the now moment,
Regardless of the circumstances of the world.
I have things to do. I know my what.
God continues to provide the how
With unlimited opportunities and resources.

Sometimes in surprising, unexpected ways,
And yes, even in the midst of the pandemic!
This time is another
Be-careful-what-you-ask-for lesson.
Yes, I did get what I asked for—
An opportunity to earn enough money
To pay a year's taxes and insurance on my house.
But at what cost?

I wandered 40 days in the wilderness
As a supervisor with the Census Bureau.
I never lost sight of
My calling, purpose, or mission,
But I created inner disharmony
By allowing myself to become money-driven
With seven-day work-weeks of 11 to 18 hour days.

It was an experience of going from
Border-line social isolation
To being dramatically over-peopled
And back to the social isolation of living alone
In the comfort of my home to contemplate
The changes in the world and in my life
During this ongoing experience of a pandemic.

I find that, on the gratitude scale,
I think less about what I do not have
And am more appreciative of what I have,
Especially in my connections with people.

I relearned that it isn't the same people
I've helped in the past who come forward to help me.
That's not the way the Law of Attraction works.
But what I give, does come back from someone.

I think more about the power of mindful thinking,
Affirmative prayers for protection,
And my responsibility for being
The human face, heart, voice, hands, and feet of God
By taking positive actions to fulfill my mission.
Each day I consciously make more phone calls,
Write more letters, send more cards,
And I'm grateful for the ones I receive.
They nourish my soul.

And in my reflective quiet moments at night,
I meditate about the question,
Is it a miracle or is it a normal manifestation
Of my belief in and my practice of
God's universal principles as taught by Unity
That I, at an age labeled medically vulnerable,
Maintain my wholeness of body, mind, and spirit
In the midst of the COVID-19 pandemic?
Either way, I accept it in awe as a gift from God
Because wholeness is my divine inheritance.

And my 40 days in the wilderness?
According to the metaphysical interpretation,
Two things were happening simultaneously.

The wilderness represents undisciplined thoughts.
In today's language? Stress and more stress
Even though I unceasingly prayed on the run!

The 40 days represents completeness.
I disciplined my thoughts. In today's language?
I did my job—fulfilled my mission
To empower others to fulfill their missions.
Specifically, to be a part of team-building
For putting together a workable infrastructure.

I knew my job was done when I was told,
"You built the railroad. Now let's see
If we can keep the train on the track without you."
It was time to release and let go.
I handed in my smartphone and ipad!

So no more drama.
I'm back to my usual centered self,
A wiser person secure in my Truth that,
At no time during this pandemic experience,
Have I been or will I be isolated or deprived
Because I AM never isolated from God!
Therefore, I AM neither lonely or alone
Because I no longer
Entertain the thought of loss
For any life situation.
I learn! I grow! I thrive! I win!
And so it is. Thank You, God

ABOUT THE AUTHOR

Jenny Johnson

Jenny Johnson, Native of Germany, moved to the US in 1997, joined East Bay Church of Religious Science, became a member of EBCRS International Choir. As a practitioner of Science of Mind, I co-facilitated the Inner Child Healing Journey with Rev. David Jones at Lovelock Prison, NV. Additional: Prison ministry: St. Quentin, CA, death row

Influencers: Ernest Holmes (Founder of Religious Science), Rev. Dr. Michael Beckwith,

Rev. Dr. Eloise Oliver, Rev. Ishmael Tetteh, Etherean Mission, Accra, Ghana.

Primary (Healing-) Work: Massage Therapy (Acupressure/Shiatsu), Reiki and clinical Hypnotherapy.

I was the sole caregiver for my only daughter (RIP) for almost 9 years, a labor of LOVE!

Although a Poet, I am writing my first book /Autobiography.

SIX

Intuition, The Voice of God

By Jenny Johnson

I believe Spiritual Awakening happens gradually over the course of Life, every single experience and hardship having an impact on the journey. Letting go of Ego and allowing Spirit to lead me into the Life already prepared for me, leads to a positive spiritual transformation.

Walking with Spirit, trusting my intuition — the voice of God — has never failed me!

In the following text I will use the words: God, Spirit, Intuition and Higher Power interchangeably.

Growing up in a household of seven — grandparents, parents and two older siblings — I was the only one in my family who had a relationship with a Higher Power. I believed strongly that I had a "Father in Heaven," somebody with a great Love for me, somebody who cared for me, strengthened and watched over me. Even through being teased by my entire family, I stood my ground and was always in touch with my inner voice.

I made my decision to move from Germany to the United States after Spirit talked to me in a dream in November of 1996. In that dream, I was leaving my country with two suitcases. I woke up in a state of bliss. I was not worried about anything, knowing that my intuition gives me instructions of what to do, and leads me on the path that was meant for me. I followed my intuition. In February of 1997, bold and brave, I moved from my country at the age of 39 to a whole different continent without any fear, trusting that I will have the blissful life I felt after waking up from my dream.

I learned through many difficult experiences that my intuition, the voice of God, always takes care of every single detail, leading me exactly where I need to be.

I was single, had never been to California before, did not know a single person there and my English was not particularly good. After landing in San Francisco, I asked the cab driver to bring me to an inexpensive hotel and found myself in the middle of the Tenderloin, which was a very "bad" area, but truly inexpensive.

Every morning I asked my Higher Power for guidance and explored the city. To have a little feeling of luxury, I normally would go into one of the big hotels and have tea or just used their powder room to freshen up. Because I was not familiar with the bus system, I walked the first few days around the city for many hours, up and down those amazing "Streets of San Francisco." It was a great adventure! I was incredibly happy and proud of myself! I felt very secure, even in this neighborhood. The other "guests" in this small hotel were residents there and admired my fearless spirit. They gave me good advice on how to stay safe in the neighborhood, and I thanked my Higher Power for "paving my way" with angels.

Very soon, I picked up some free newspapers like the <u>Guardian</u> and learned to read the abbreviations in the rental section. I made a few phone calls and found an inexpensive apartment in Oakland, CA. The owner of the apartment complex was German, and his wife was a lady from Switzerland. They had already rented out the apartment they had advertised in the paper. We chatted a little while on the phone, and they invited me to come and see them, if I should be in their area. I made some more calls and had two appointments the next day to see some apartments in Oakland, CA. I took BART (Bay Area Rapid Transit) to Oakland and found out that the two apartments were right around the corner of the German landlord I spoke to the day before. After seeing the two apartments, which were too expensive and had requirements that I could not fulfill, I stopped by the complex owned by the German couple. They were a very friendly older couple, age wise like my parents. They were very excited to speak German again, and invited me to a Japanese restaurant for lunch. Impressed by my story and bravery, they decided to rent a one-bedroom furnished unit in the basement to me. They had fixed up this unit for themselves, in case they had to stay there overnight for any reason

I learned in retrospect that when *following my inner voice and trusting it, everything is prepared and ready! What is meant to be, to fulfill "The Story of my Life" is always available for me!*

In any situation, if I have any questions, if I am confused about what to do, I will still myself and ask Spirit. I know the answers are always right within me. I have learned not to rely on my own understanding. *I trust in my inner voice. Spirit within knows all the answers and will lead me along the right path.*

The other day I was missing my glasses, I started to look everywhere. In my backyard, in my front yard, on my lanai, in every room in the house. I went through the trash, I looked in the refrigerator, in the pantry, in the laundry basket, in the garage, even in places where I have not been for days, but I could not find my glasses. I was frantic! I needed my glasses to see far and to drive. I stayed home the whole day because I could not drive anywhere. I was looking again and again and again in the same places. Then I texted a neighbor and asked if she could come over the next day to help me search. I was exhausted.

The next morning, after waking up, I started to look again, but then I decided to ask my inner voice! I sat on the lanai and did a breathing technique that I learned a long time ago, before I went into a prayer and meditation. I asked spirit to lead me to my glasses. After my prayer and meditation, I felt confident, and so I let it be for a moment. I went out into my backyard to take a swim in the pool. While I was swimming, I remembered that the day before I took some photos of my plants in the backyard. When I take photos with my camera, I usually take my glasses off and clip them to the front of my T shirt or blouse.

I got out of the pool and walked towards the first plant that I remembered taking a photo of, and there in the mulch and dirt were my glasses!

I learned that I do not have to exhaust myself even with small things, all I have to do is *be still and ask my inner voice to lead me, guide me and provide for me.*

A few days ago, while riding my bike, I heard something behind me breathing. It was a pit bull chasing me. I have always been afraid of that kind of dog...There it was, without a leash, and without an owner, chasing me on my bike. My first instinct was to ride faster, but I knew that I could not out-ride him. I slowed down and stopped, got off my bike, and looked into his face. I raised my finger and told him in a sharp voice to sit. To my surprise he sat right away, and I almost laughed, because I saw that he was shaking by the tone of my voice.

This is exactly what I need to do in everyday life.

Fear and faith cannot co-exist, so I choose faith!

Standing tall in every situation of life can be accomplished by tapping into the Truth of who we are and claiming the Christ qualities (Spirit/intuition) within us.

I can live at ease; Spirit is the true force in my life.

I moved to Florida a little over two years ago. I do not have family in the US and all my friends are in California. After moving into my new home, I felt a little lonely. I started to travel a little bit, flew to New York, spent a week in the Bahamas and The Dominican Republic. I took daytrips to Naples, Punta Gorda, Tarpon Springs and a few times went to Orlando/ Disney World. Every time I was gone, eating out in restaurants I felt sick.

I was diagnosed with diverticulitis at the end of 2018. I had to change my diet, prepare and eat my food at home. I learned how to separate carbs from protein, found a tea and supplements to help with pain, heartburn and other discomforts. I stocked up my pantry with healthy items, many new herbs and spices, and became quite good in cooking delicious flavorful food. I let go of ten pounds in no time. I enjoyed riding my bicycle, swimming in my pool and doing some yoga at home.

All of that was positive, but I hardly ever had company. Socializing over food is a major way to connect with family and friends, that mostly happens in restaurants… and then COVID 19 hit! I did not have to adjust to staying away from people, I was already doing this for over a year! I was used to being alone at home, cooking at home, exercising and enjoying my beautiful home and tropical backyard!!! In the meantime, I became vegan, 100% plant-based, took on the hobby of photography, created amazing plant-based dishes and took photos of them. I am working on my first cookbook. I still ride my bike and take pictures of this beautiful wildlife around my neighborhood. Gators as well as birds, butterflies, squirrels and plants became my friends and we do not have to wear masks!!! I am no longer lonely, too busy with my beautiful hobbies.

I am staying positive in my approach to life. I have not watched the news in twenty three years. What I need to know, will come to me, I do not have to look for it! While others are posting disturbing numbers, and panic-inducing articles, I am posting pictures of beautiful sunsets in my neighborhood or publishing my newest plant-based recipes.

When I try to resolve things on my own, I almost lose my mind, trying to control things I do not have control over. At times, I get so exhausted and frustrated by life's demands and negative influences on this planet, that I become depressed or experience anxiety.

When I start to feel this way, I remember God's goodness, and trust God to resolve everything that is concerning me. I have developed a spiritual practice, that I follow to avoid feeling depressed or having anxiety. Here is a peek into my spiritual toolbox:

After awakening in the morning, I drink water, turn on relaxing music, either meditation music or sounds of nature, I have a fountain in my backyard and I sit on my lanai reading the Daily Word, or other spiritual inspirational publications. Listening to the sounds of nature, I relax and meditate on the words of wisdom I have just read. I find it particularly important to dedicate this time right after awakening to my spiritual practice, this way my day can unfold in peace and harmony, in joy and happiness. I am strengthened by my inner voice and it helps me maneuver through all situations of life

Many times, I pick up a pen and write my own devotionals, which develop during the meditation. They are the words of my inner wisdom.

Knowing that Spirit is within me, I have Peace in my heart, Joy in my soul and much gratitude for my life.

Another highly effective spiritual tool is to speak out words of gratitude every morning and every evening before going to sleep. I focus on what I am grateful for, this way thoughts of negativity do not even enter my mind. Prayer, meditation and positive affirmations are my three go-to spiritual "healers". Some examples: I am love, I am peace, I am joy, I am success, I am wise, I am grateful, I am blessed, I am health, I am happy, I am worthy… This helps me to feel confident, knowing the Truth: *I am a spiritual being having a human experience. That human experience can be wonderful by remembering who I AM, letting go and letting GOD!*

When I look back on the many negative experiences in my life, and delve into them, I can see the "silver lining" or the lesson, that the Universe has taught me.

I call this THE STORY vs. THE ESSENCE:

The Story:

Every morning around 7 am I go for a bike ride in my neighborhood. Most of the time, my neighbor G. would be out there with her bike as well, and we ride together and chat a little.

One morning G. was riding ahead of me and I was very close behind her. When we reached a neighbor's house with a beautifully designed driveway, I pointed it out to G. She was looking over to the right, slightly moving in the direction I pointed out and I t-boned her bike and flew over both of our bicycles. Long story short…I broke my elbow, and the ligaments in my wrist were torn. In severe pain, I pushed my bike home, cleaned the blood from my knees and inside my hands, sat for a minute and asked the Universe what to do. I was all alone, in pain and with possible broken bones. I reached out for a LYFT ride, an app that I installed years earlier on my phone, when I did not have a car. When I moved to Florida, I heard of an Urgent Care in my neighborhood, stored their phone number in my phone, following my intuition. They patched me up, took an x-ray and put my elbow in a sling, helped me make an appointment with an orthopedic doctor for the next day, prescribed pain medication and ordered the pharmacy to deliver to my house! A friend from Sarasota came that same afternoon, helped me out of my clothes and put me in my night gown, prepared meals for the next two days, and even picked up my meds, since the pharmacy did not have a deliverer that day. Even though it was not easy to get help in the next 3 months, I became stronger and more inventive with helping myself while only using one arm.

I met a man online a few months prior to that accident. We talked on the phone and Face Timed a couple of times, but just found that our friendship would not lead into a relationship. We decided we were living too far apart to make it work. We stopped the contact all together about one week before my bike accident. I was saddened. Then I began to worry. I had some sleepless nights, and my thoughts were playing tricks on me. I kept thinking, "*I am always alone… I don't have anyone to care for me… What if something happens to me, an accident, a stroke…???*"

The Essence:

Those questions — put out in the Universe — were answered very quickly!

I am never alone… Spirit takes care of me… No matter what – God is in control!!!

What I fear – I will attract! What I focus my energy on, I will have more of! Worrying is not trusting GOD!

Ever since then, I break down my experiences in The Story vs. The Essence or The Story vs. The Truth… The story is long and complicated, full of drama and negative believes, the Essence is simple, clear and true…

It helps me to see the positive in everything and to trust and not to worry. Most importantly to let go of control and leave it to GOD.

I learned to surrender, to trust, to relax, knowing Spirit in me knows the answers.

Every day is a new learning experience and with every situation I can open my spiritual toolbox.

Words of one of my favorite songs come to mind:
"you don't have to worry, and don't you be afraid…
Joy comes in the morning, troubles they don't last always,
For there's a friend in Spirit, who will wipe your tears away –
And if your heart is broken, just lift your hands and say:
Oh, I know that I can make it, I know that I can stand,
No matter what may come my way,
MY LIFE'S IN SPIRIT'S HANDS

ABOUT THE AUTHOR

Jennifer "Revel" Johnston

Jennifer grew up in New England. Travel is her passion. She has trekked in the Himalayas, visited historical sites in the Greek Islands, and stargazed in the Australian Outback. She earned a Master of Public Health from University of North Carolina at Chapel Hill. Her career is dedicated to improving the health of communities to support well-being for all. When Jennifer discovered it was possible to live in eternal summer she moved to Florida. The natural and artistic beauty of Sarasota make it home. Jennifer is happy to be a member of Center for Spiritual Living Cultural Coast.

SEVEN

Taking the Leap

By Jennifer "Revel" Johnston

I tried to take an afternoon nap to recover from my overnight flight. I was too excited to sleep. I was in Arcidosso! The quaint, Tuscan, hillside town (complete with a medieval castle) awaited exploration.

I strolled down to a little park in the center of town, sat on a bench with my journal, and wondered what exactly I would write during this writing retreat. A feather in mid-air caught my eye. It floated down, wafted across the park, and landed on the bench right beside me. It felt like a message but I wasn't sure what it meant. I was on an Italian eat, pray, write adventure and I looked forward to being guided by Spirit.

How did I arrive here?

A few years earlier, I googled "spiritual places near me," seeking guidance. I began walking labyrinths, going to retreat centers near my home in Florida, and meditating daily. My greatest desire was, and is, to live in the flow of life, at peace and in constant connection with my Creator. I visited the Center for Spiritual Living, which met in a high school near my house on Sunday mornings. The first time I attended a service, the minister gave a talk on how a chick is hatched.

The tiny creature chips away at the inside of its shell. Eventually, it works long enough and hard enough to stretch beyond its current container and bursts forth into the unknown.

The minister asked, "what compels a chick to break out of its shell?"

It happens when the chick becomes so confined and uncomfortable it risks everything, destroying its only home, and emerges into a new world, where it can grow unhampered. It is a similar discomfort to outgrow one's current situation and it drives humans to seek enlarged horizons.

This scenario of unexpected change showed up in my life when I turned forty. I interviewed for a dream job in a different city. The position was the perfect combination of my previous roles, with a highly-respected organization that would allow me to do what I love—improve the well-being of communities. I was enthusiastic about the possibilities, but nervous at the prospect of moving away from the city I loved and had lived in for eleven years. I was ready for a professional leap, but not a personal one. How could I leave my large circle of friends, my new spiritual community, and the first home I owned, to move to a place I never anticipated living?

I was offered the coveted job opportunity and I accepted. Within two weeks, I found a rental condo and was moving to Sarasota, Florida. In the three years since my relocation, I have worked with mentors, been pushed outside my comfort zone, and been inspired creatively. Now, I can see that when this job appeared, I was ready to expand my horizons. By following my intuition, I landed in just the right place. Sometimes, we don't realize how small our comfort zone has become until we take a leap and look back at it from a different perspective.

Within several months of my move, change showed up out of the blue. The tenant in my beloved first home received a job transfer and I listed it for rent, again. I received a message from my former neighbor—a realtor— who saw my advertisement. She had a potential buyer who would like to see the house. I explained that I planned to keep it as a rental property. It was the only place I had ever lived where I wasn't a renter. I saw it as a potential source of income and liked the idea of having a place to go back to, in the city that felt like home.

Being a landlord is tough. In my first six months, a hurricane grazed our area and the tenant requested to move early. Being a good realtor, my neighbor emphasized the fact that it was a seller's market. For the right price, everything's for sale. Right? So, I agreed to a showing the next day. Within twenty-four hours I received a written offer. I never intended to sell my home, yet opportunity knocked.

I went for a walk on Siesta Key Beach to gain clarity. With sand quartz beneath my feet and the sound of waves lapping the shore two things came into focus in my mind. First, the big picture; my tenant wanted to move out and a potential buyer wanted to move in. I wanted to move forward with making Sarasota my home. All four parties were women—owner, tenant, buyer, and realtor. These exciting roles were not available for women just a few generations ago. My single mom never purchased or sold a home.

Secondly, in my short time in Sarasota, I had changed. I dived into learning a fast-paced job and a new community. I was fully committed to enjoying it. With nothing on my social calendar, I explored parks and attended concerts in solitude. I tried new spiritual practices, including sound healing and energy healing. I enrolled in workshops at spiritual centers and went to kirtans for the first time where I was uplifted by the chanting, dancing crowd. I joined a writing group that engaged in dialogue on the page, asking Spirit, or meaningful guides in our lives, for insight.

When the chance to sell my first home showed up, I surprised myself and my friends by accepting the offer. I was ready to release my ties to my old neighborhood and the good times I had there. It was a decision of the heart, made with ease. I could see the benefits for all involved in the potential transaction. I realized that my intentions over the past months, inviting in new and fun experiences, allowed me to show up differently when this offer arrived. My lack of attachment to the past, willingness to stretch beyond what I know, and trust in Divine timing created a new possibility.

At one point in the sale process, when the tenant was gone and the buyer's financing almost fell through, listening to Wayne Dyer's affirmations helped me to stay open—trusting the highest and best was unfolding for everyone involved. I faced the fear of financial uncertainty and held steady. My decision-making muscles were strong, after navigating a big move on a short timeline and embracing a completely new life.

Living in a new place brings an adjustment period. Sarasota is a much smaller community than I am used to and my new professional role is more public. The condo I moved into had upstairs neighbors that did not share my love of peace and quiet. So, when my lease was up, I rented a different unit in the same building. It's on the top floor with a view of tree tops and the sunset. Making new friends takes time, so I spent many weekends on my own, walking the beach and sightseeing. I deeply related to that first message I heard at the Center for Spiritual Living. Like a chick, life propelled me beyond a situation that had become too small, to spread my wings and venture out to explore a new environment.

The leader of my writing group surprised us during one session with an invitation to go to Tuscany on a writing retreat. I hadn't been to Europe in twenty years and had never gone on a writing retreat. I didn't think of myself as a writer, though I've always enjoyed writing. I immediately raised my hand and said yes. I wanted to visit Tuscany and try on the role of writer for the first time. As I prepared for the trip, I noticed a picture of Ca' d'Zan on my Vision Board, the Italian-style former home of John and Mable Ringling. It's open to the public and is one of my favorite spots in Sarasota. I was headed to Italy to immerse myself in similar views.

The beauty of Tuscany and its people infused my writing. The words flowed easily and told the stories of my life. I wrote under golden autumn foliage and in medieval churches. I savored fresh, flavorful food and long walks in the countryside. Our group called ourselves sunflowers and developed soul to soul connections sharing our writing and walking arm-in-arm down winding streets under a full moon. I wrote in my journal, "I revel in my intuition, sing my song, ask for what I need, and declare myself open to receive."

Before returning home, I stopped in Paris to sightsee on my own. I felt called to visit Chartres Cathedral and took a train there early one morning. The powerful structure holds the energy of centuries of pilgrims. I took off my shoes and walked the labyrinth. My bare feet absorbed the cold of the well-worn limestone. I retraced the journey of my life until I reached the center. I toured the Crypt, where pilgrims used to symbolically travel through a womb before climbing interior steps into the cathedral, emerging from darkness into the spiritual world, filled with the bright colors and beauty of stained-glass windows. I went outside and took breaks from the intense energy of the cathedral to ground myself. It is a massive work of devotion to the Divine on our material plane. I walked to town for lunch mid-day, taking the same route I walked that morning. Somehow, I found myself on a street I hadn't seen before. I was the only one in sight and it was covered with white feathers. I felt light and assured that God is always in view. I wrote, "I'm in the right place at the right time."

Throughout my life there have been many times I trusted my inner voice, took a risk, and discovered an opportunity for growth. I continue to reap the benefits of saying yes to life when new horizons present themselves. I am uplifted by the philosophy of Ernest Holmes who urged us to be open to a new thought. Holmes taught the practice of praying to affirm there is one Source of all life and I am a magnificent part of that life. I am the one who creates my experiences, and with gratitude and trust in the goodness of creation, my possibilities are limitless. My new spiritual community in Sarasota affirms my inner knowing that life is seeking to flow through me and the truest response is to surrender to the eternal calling toward wholeness and harmony. Holmes' said, "to live by inspiration means to sense the divine touch in everything, to enter into the spirit of things, to enter into the joy of living." My forties are giving me the chance to do just that.

The leap that landed me here ushered in a fruitful season of personal growth. I am in a spiritual place. My life used to be outwardly focused on who and what needed my attention- friends, family, work, dating. I invested a lot of time and effort into searching for fulfillment outside of myself. Now, I consciously direct my energy into maintaining an inner sense of peace and creativity. For the first time, I have a healthy balance of work, rest, and play which allows me to feel inspired and act from my true self. My priority is becoming the fullest expression of unconditional love and light in all circumstances.

Since returning from the writing retreat, I notice feathers on my path now and then and they feel like a nudge from Spirit. Recently, on my morning walk, I looked down to find a long, white feather with a black tip resting in front of me. It felt like a clear sign that spending time appreciating nature and nurturing myself has put me on the right path. That evening, during my monthly session with my spiritual coach she opened by saying, I'm hearing a message from the Divine, "you're right where you are supposed to be." And my heart knows it to be true.

ABOUT THE AUTHOR

Caroline Robertie

Caroline Robertie, was born in Hertfordshire, England, Caroline credits the peace of the English countryside, and books from a small traveling library with the start of her spiritual quest. "The Story of Albert Schweitzer" and his reverence for life, Viktor Frankl's "Man's Search For Meaning," Plato, Socrates, and "The Complete Works of Carl Jung" shaped those early years. Raised as a Christian, she knew there was more. With a degree in Business Administration, she worked in London and New York never letting go of her quest. The freedom and joy of realizing we are all one, and there is only One, brought her to Sarasota in 2019. Her search continues...

EIGHT

THANKSGIVING

By Caroline Robertie

Jennifer Jane was born November 23, 1969. She was the first girl born on my husband's side of the family since 1853. Jennie had blonde, curly hair that sparkled in the sunlight, and a mischievous, happy disposition. When she was just two years old, I went to wake her from her nap and found her lying very still and not breathing. All efforts by me and by the Rescue Squad failed to revive her. I was later told that sepsis, caused by a malfunctioning kidney valve, had spread to her diaphragm which then prevented her lungs from working. Suddenly, without warning, just like that, she was gone. It was devastating. Only that morning we had played by the brook that ran through our property and she had seemed fine. How could she not be with me? I had everything to offer her and I loved my little girl so much. Our son, who was four years old, started nursery school two weeks after her death and now, there I sat in our old Victorian house in the New Jersey countryside, alone with my sadness.

My tears overflowed like a swollen river onto my daily journal as I struggled in conversations with God about where I was spiritually, trying to make sense of it all. Jennie's footprints were still in the sand where we had played just the day before and I dreaded the rain that would surely come and take them away. Grateful for my Christian upbringing. I had so many questions, especially about pain, guilt, suffering and now loss. Had I done something wrong to make God mad at me? After all, I had been taught that God was a God of love. What does that mean? Was He really watching for my mistakes so that He could punish me for them?

Seeking answers, I delved into spiritual books. There must be a reason why this happened, and I was determined to find it. Having taken Greek in school I bought a *Greek Interlinear Bible* and decided I would translate the *New Testament* for myself because surely some of it had been mistranslated by men with egos and I could find my answers there. I devoured Carl Jung's works; Viktor Frankl's *Man's Search for Meaning* and how he was able to rise above the darkness of unspeakable horror in Nazi death camps; Marcus Bach who spoke of finding a oneness with all life and an awareness of the unseen in his book *The Power of Perception.* I sought answers in every book I could lay my hands on, trying to make sense of it all. Jacob Boehme stated in *The Whispering Self* that "The moment you begin to seek, you have already found, for you have set your feet upon the path."

After coming to the United States to work in New York at the age of 19, I had joined the Episcopal Church. There were no Bibles in the pews, so I tried the Baptist Church. There, I found less focus on guilt and punishment and more on mission work. I continued my quest, seeking for answers by volunteering in Central America, Puerto Rico, the Dominican Republic, and Haiti. I tried the Fundamental Church because they had an amazing project with Aids orphans in a remote Zulu village in South Africa and volunteered there several years in a row, loving these people who lived in abject poverty under the remnants of Apartheid. How could they have such joy and love for God on their faces? Once more, I questioned why a loving God would allow this?

A year after Jennie's death, Jessica was born. I was so happy to have another girl. It was hard living in the house where Jennie had died, so we moved to Cape Cod and lived for many happy years in a sprawling, 1857 Sea Captain's house by the sea. The sound of the ocean, walks on the beach, late evenings sitting in the sand dunes watching the moon rise all restored my soul.

Jessica had the same blonde hair and blue eyes as Jennie and was active in ballet and theater. She graduated from college with a nursing degree, met and married a handsome, dark haired doctor and moved to Colorado. But Jennie was always with me, especially on birthdays and anniversaries when I wept, and wondered where she was, searching for her in shooting stars and butterflies, always asking why, and my quest for answers continued.

On a Saturday morning in July 2004, my husband came out of the shower, threw his arms around me and said, "I love you so much. The boys and I are going fishing today, what are you doing?" "I think I'm going to go for a walk along the beach," I said, "Bring me back a whole one and I'll cook it on the grill for dinner."

And that was the last time I saw him.

I returned from my walk to find a message from the Coast Guard on my phone. My husband had collapsed at the wheel of the boat and was being taken to Cape Cod Hospital. "It's very grave," they said. They would not tell me more and I knew in my heart he was dead. I called my kids and drove as slowly as I could to the hospital, not wanting to face what was surely waiting for me.

Just like that. He was gone. Suddenly, without any warning. How could that be? Only this morning we had hugged each other. We had had a great week together; his last words were "I love you;" we had had a good, long marriage; raised two beautiful children; had more fun and adventures together; and I knew he died doing what he loved, at sea with his friends and with the wind in his hair. Nothing was left unsaid or undone. In some sense, I felt a certain peace in my heart. But the grief that I had managed to suppress for all those years once again raised its ugly head.

Alone now, I was thrust back into the arms of God, searching for answers. I retreated into solitude. The days would dawn and end in silence and I would pour my heart out into my journal trying to make sense of it all, to understand who this God is. But at the end of the day, coming home to a dark house, an empty chair, and no one to share my day and my thoughts with, ate away at my peace and I remember saying to myself, "Is this it?"

A few months later, I received a call from my son-in-law in Colorado. My darling daughter Jessica, who had been given pain medication after injuring her back lifting a heavy patient, was now addicted to the medication and he had arranged for her to go to rehab. Over the next four years, and two attempts at treatment, she was still struggling. One day, she phoned me to say her husband had asked her for a divorce and told her to move out with their two small daughters. I decided I would rent an apartment in Boulder for six months so that she and the girls could move in with me and I could be there to support them. I was terrified of losing her. I had no way of controlling anything and did not know how much more I could take.

Sometimes, when the rug seems to be pulled out from under our feet, we have no place to turn to but God, so again I devoured books and argued with God every morning in my journal. I was not sure I could survive any more loss and felt as if I were at the bottom of a deep pit with no way to climb out.

We had been in the apartment for a few weeks and it was Thanksgiving week, and I did not feel at all like giving thanks. In fact, I could not think of anything to be thankful for. Thanksgiving. For what? It would have been my late husband's birthday November 21st, Jennie's birthday November 23rd, and now I was losing another daughter? Exactly why was I supposed to be thankful?

As I tried to act normal in the kitchen to prepare a traditional turkey dinner with all the trimmings and put on a happy face for the children, I felt overwhelmed with sadness. The future looked bleak. Despite my searching, I had found no answers. I decided to take a walk before dinner to clear my head.

It was a misty, fall Colorado day. I walked along a trail near Boulder Creek which ran swiftly like a wide river through Boulder after tumbling down from the mountains. Presently, I could see a gentle, sloping, mossy bank beneath giant cottonwood trees. I cut through a field of soft grass and discovered that the mossy bank led down to the water's edge. The last of the leaves in the trees rattled in the breeze above. They were as dead and dry as I felt. I sat down and buried my head in my hands and sobbed my heart out. Why God, oh why? I missed my daughter Jennie so much. My husband and I had had a deep love for each other. Why was everything I loved taken from me?

Right there, by the river, I let God have it! Shaking my fist to the sky I yelled as loudly as I could, reciting a litany of my woes. "You've taken my baby, you've taken my husband, and now I'm losing my other daughter! Why don't you just burn my house down while you are at it?" I must have gone on like that for several minutes as I raised my voice above the sound of the water. It felt good to let it all out, and I sat there, panting to regain my breath.

Totally spent, feeling utterly sorry for myself, I dabbed my tears and looked up. The sun was sparkling like diamonds on the surface of the water and there, not 25 feet away from me, a homeless man lay asleep on a piece of cardboard. He did not stir, yet he must have heard everything I said. I looked at that man and thought to myself, this man has nothing; and I have everything. Then I started to list what I did have to be thankful for: I had my health, I had a roof over my head, I had enough food to eat, a car to get around in, grown children and beautiful grandchildren. I had friends and family who loved me, I had plenty of clothes, enough money to get by on and a spiritual community to support me. The list went on and on. In fact, it took me longer to list what I had than it had taken to complain about what I lacked.

Aware that I was alone, and not wanting to disturb this man, I rose to my feet and walked quietly away through the fields to my apartment. I was aware that something had changed within me. In the midst of fear, loss and sadness, I was giving thanks. How could that be?

The Course in Miracles says, "Seek not to change the world but choose to change your mind about the world." In a moment, my perception had changed simply because my thoughts had changed. I realized that yes, I cannot control the world around me or how other people behave, but I can control how I see and think about it.

My spirit lifted and my pace quickened as I set off eagerly to join my daughter and granddaughters for Thanksgiving dinner, to embrace them and give thanks together.

Without my intention, somehow my mind and outlook had changed. What if I could in the future deliberately decide to change my mind about things. Would it work? I vowed to try next time the opportunity arose.

On an unusually warm Saturday afternoon in early December, I decided to go for a hike up Shadow Canyon to the top of Bear Mountain, an 8,500 ft. peak in the Foothills of the Rocky Mountains which loomed above the city of Boulder. With the busy Holiday Season approaching, I was eager to find some solitude, to ponder all I had been through in the last few months.

I set off through wide expanses of tall grass dotted with scrub pine trees. After a couple of miles, I reached the foot of Shadow Canyon, aptly named because being on the lee side of the mountain it rarely sees the sunshine. The deep silence was broken only by the sound of a mountain stream and the squawking of birds flying high above. As I trod carefully up the steep slopes, I could hear voices on the trail far behind me. The sounds got louder and louder as they approached, disturbing my solitude. I paused to let them pass. Soon, another group of hikers came by, laughing and chatting. I decided to sit on the trunk of a fallen tree beside the trail to have a snack and drink of water to allow some distance between us so I could continue in silence. I was no sooner back on the trail when I could hear even louder voices approaching. I was getting annoyed. All I wanted was to be alone in the wilderness with my thoughts. Don't these people appreciate nature? I stepped aside to allow a dozen or more college students to hike by. They were talking and laughing so loudly about their studies they did not even notice me as they passed.

Once again, the sound of voices slowly disappeared. I was alone with my thoughts in the deep silence of the canyon forest, cliffs rising sharply on either side of me to the small patch of blue sky above. What would happen, I wondered, if instead of being irritated by all these people I changed my mind and said to myself, "Isn't it marvelous that on a Saturday afternoon, when there is a college football game, these students are not in their dorms drinking beer and watching TV but have set themselves the challenge of climbing Bear Mountain and enjoying the Rocky Mountains."

It seemed as if a weight had been lifted from my shoulders. I could not wait to continue my climb and see how far those kids had managed to make it. Up, and up I went, finally emerging from the shadows to the ridge and open sky and the path that led to the top. I stopped to fill an empty water bottle with the last of the wild raspberries that had escaped the bears which feed on them before hibernation and continued on my way.

As I scrambled over the large rocks that must be scaled to reach the peak, I could again hear voices. It was the group of students sitting on the top of the mountain, raising their arms in victory, shouting, and celebrating their achievement. How wonderful, I thought. Far below, the city seemed tiny and beyond it the Plains that faded endlessly to the East. Eagles and vultures swooped in the air below, carried on the wind. I was happy. Happy with myself for completing the climb; and pleased to celebrate with such a fine group of young people. Indeed, by deciding to change my thoughts and my mind something was different and my whole outlook was different.

I do not know why, on that Thanksgiving Day, I had not noticed the homeless man by the river before, or where he came from. But seeing him at just the right moment was truly a blessing and had somehow opened the eyes of my heart. Jesus is quoted in The Gospel of Mark as saying, "You have eyes, but you do not see." The Greek word used for "see" can also mean to perceive or understand. Now I saw, I understood.

Could it be that Spirit has the answers for us all the time, but we are generally too busy with our own plans, our own efforts to control and our own thoughts, to see or understand. Eric Butterworth said, "Change your life by changing your thoughts," and that is exactly what had happened to me.

I conclude with a poem by R.H. Grenville which I found many years ago in the book, *The Power of Perception*, by Marcus Bach:

Oh, let my eyes be opened wide
That I may clearly see,
How often in another's guise
God walks the road with me.

ABOUT THE AUTHOR

Jerry Stricker

Jerry Stricker was born in Newport, KY. He graduated from The University of KY where he majored in accounting. He passed the Certified Public Accounting test the same year he graduated from college. His first job was with Arthur Young & Co., CPA's firm. After six years, he joined Gradison & Co, a member firm of the New York Stock Exchange.

He spent 25 years with Gradison as an Executive Vice President and Chief Financial Officer. His daughter Kim made her transition two years after he retired. He now resides in Sarasota and is a member of the Unity of Sarasota.

NINE

How I Overcame, Survived, and Learned to Have Peace With the Passing of My Daughter, Kim

By Jerry Stricker

M y story starts on January 23, 1968 when my wife and I adopted Kimberly Ann Stricker, who was born on January 16, 1968 and was only seven days old when we adopted her. Kim was a beautiful daughter and highly intelligent. She graduated with Honors from high school, she graduated with a B.A. of Education with High Distinction from University of Kentucky and was Recipient of Sara Guerin Scholarship for student teaching in Christ Church, New Zealand. Her postgraduate studies were in Speech Language Pathology at University of Cincinnati. Kim loved children and her graduate degree program was speech pathology for children. She was a University of Kentucky Fellow. In 1997, the University of Kentucky built a new library on campus. Without my knowledge, UK named a study room after my daughter, called the Kim Stricker Room.

Kim and I spent a lot of time together, including travel in America, New Zealand, Mexico, and Europe. Kim also spent a lot of time with her mother, her sister Melanie, and her brother Jeff. On October 27, 1994 I received the phone call that no parent wants, from my former wife. She told me that "Kim died." I said I will be right over. I was in shock and after a few blocks driving my car, I started crying. When I got there, in addition to my former wife, was my son, daughter, Presbyterian minister and our pediatrician who was a family friend. The minister said if I only would have insisted that Kim come for therapy. I said to the minister no one should blame themselves for what happened tonight. I felt then and still do that no one should feel guilty. During my many years of grief, the word "why" was never important to me. One of my friends, who worked at a funeral home, told me that it was very unusual to not want to know why someone died by suicide. What was important is I could not physically see her, have a conversation with her or walk her down the aisle someday.

No parent wants to bury their child. What do you do after your child has made their transition? I cried a lot, it did not matter where I was or who I was with, I cried. There were many other things to do. We planned her memorial services. One for the extended family, cousins, my siblings, etc. and one for everyone else. After the services we had a reception at the church so our friends could express their condolences. Since Kim did not have a will, I met with a local Judge who appointed me to be the executor of her estate. She left each of her family a suicide note. In her notes, she said she loved each one of us, but could not deal with her depression. None of her family knew she had depression. She hid it from us. In Kim's note she left me; she wanted a friend's daughter to receive $1,000 when she turned 18-years-old. This is another example of her love of children. I set up a saving account for the bequest and she did receive the money when she turned 18.

During the first 90 days of grieving I was suicidal myself. I wanted to be with Kim. I was given books about parents who lost a child. Family and friends would do their best to help me. I attended church, I prayed, and I had therapy sessions. I started attending two workshops that really helped. Compassionate Friends, a support group that helps parents survive the loss of a child. The other group was called Survivors of Suicide. During one of the sessions, the name George Anderson came up. Anderson is a psychic medium from New York City. I was told that he has the unique ability to communicate with souls on the other side. There were three books written about Anderson communicating with souls. I read all three books. Years later, I learned he was considered by other psychics as the one that every psychic wanted to emulate. In April 1995, my daughter Melanie and I had a session with Anderson. We flew to Atlanta to meet with him. He knew nothing about me or anybody else in my family. During the session, he contacted a soul and her name was Kim, my daughter. He said that Kim was sending flowers to her sister; Anderson did not know why. We told him that Melanie just had a birthday. Per Anderson, Kim said "I know Dad has been keeping remarkably busy and she was glad, because it helped him to deal with his grief." I was thinking and saying the exact same words recently. The one-hour session was very emotional. We both felt Kim's presence in the session. We were allowed and encouraged to record the session and we did. I decided that I would like to bring Anderson to Covington, KY where I lived. I talked to Anderson's agent, Andrew Barone about this and he asked me to be their agent for this session in Covington. I agreed. I let my friends know that Anderson was coming and many people all over the country found out about it. I received phone calls from people who lost a loved one. It was very therapeutic for me to talk to them. The second workshop we had was held in April 1996. My daughter Melanie and I were joined by my former wife and my daughter's future wife, Chris. One of the amazing things that we learned from the session about Kim and the other side is that people who died by suicide are isolated for a period and they have animals nearby to comfort them. In one of the sessions, Anderson told us that one of Kim's "jobs" in heaven is to welcome animals when they enter heaven. Anderson said no one who commits suicide goes to hell, because the souls have told him there is no hell. We had a third session a year later in Cincinnati. When Anderson started the session, he said Kim is with a young man who is in a military uniform and she says it is your brother and aren't you happy? I was speechless. Kim said, "duh Dad", that's what Kim would have said to me when she was alive on earth. Our family was truly fortunate to have those three sessions with a psychic. In 1999, George Anderson and Andrew Barone wrote a book titled "George Anderson's LESSONS from the LIGHT". On the acknowledgments page he expressed thanks to many people for their "contributions in word or deed": including myself and the soul of Ms. Kimberly Stricker. On Page 100 of the book he talks about Kim.

After 12 years of grieving, attending workshops, therapy sessions, reading books and having three discernments with George Anderson, I still had the thought that Kim should not have died by suicide. I started going to New Thought Unity Church in Cincinnati in 1997. In July of 2007 George Whitton, who later became a Unity Minister, suggested that I attend a workshop at the church by Reverend Martha Creek, a certified facilitator of a Byron Katie program called, "Loving What Is." I read Katie's books, which I highly recommend. Whitton knew that I was still in pain from Kim making her transition. I attended Martha's workshop and it was extremely helpful. During the balance of 2007, I attended several of Martha's workshops and retreats. In one of the classes, a student told me about a Byron Katie's Mental Cleanse workshop in Los Angeles, CA. I attended Katie's workshop and it changed my life. The workshop started the day after Christmas and ended on New Year's Day. Katie would sit on the stage and start the day with an empty chair next to her. She started at 9 am and stayed until 9 pm. We all would take lunch and dinner breaks. Each day, there would be about 300 people in the room. If you wanted to talk to Katie, you would go stand in front of a microphone and wait for her to call on you and maybe she would ask you to come and sit next to her. On the second day, Katie called on me. She asked me to tell her a little bit about myself. I told her I was an elected Covington, KY City Commissioner. Katie calls her program the WORK. She has a worksheet that you can complete, and she will ask you four questions about each answer on your worksheet. My first answer to her first question was "My daughter should not have died by suicide." She asked me is it true? Yes or No? My answer was Yes. She then asked me to come sit next to her and I did for one hour in front of 300 people. It was the most amazing hour that I ever spent in my life. A blank copy of the one-page worksheet is at the end of this story. It is also printable on Katie's web page www.thework.com. My session with Katie was recorded and after I came back to KY, I listened to the CD many times. I concluded that Kim should have died by suicide because she did. That gave me peace for the first time since October 27, 1994.

The following are some things I learned from the many life experiences and workshops that I have attended:

- All the emotional pain in my life is caused by my thoughts, only 100%. My new thought is "that Kim should have died by suicide because she did." There is no pain in that statement. It gives me peace and I could laugh and have a good time, without feeling guilty.

- I have read that many parents wonder why their friends and relatives avoid them after they suffer the loss of a child. It is not that they do not care, it is because they are unsure of what they should say. All they have to say is, "I'm sorry to hear about your loss." Do not say, "Your child is in a better place." Do not say," God only gives you what you can deal with." When someone said that to me, I thought that if I were a weaker person, my daughter Kim would still be alive.

- There are three types of businesses: God business, your business, and my business. If I get into God business, that can be incredibly stressful for me. If I get in your business, that will be stressful for both of us. What I must do is keep reminding myself to stay in my own business. Besides, my business is a full-time job.

- What also keeps me peaceful is my new belief system: "What other people think of me is none of my business."

- Our loved ones, who have made their transition, are still alive in our thoughts.

- I live in the present, the past is over, and the future is unknown. An example, I have a doctor's appointment tomorrow at 3 pm. I will not know if that is going to happen until I am in the doctor's office.

- Life does not have to be painful; trust me it does not. When someone says something about me that may not be kind, I have a choice to not get upset.

- The best thing about the past is, that it is over.

- One of the messages I learned from Reverend Martha Creek is, "we talk about Loving What Is; when something bad happens, you don't have to love it and you don't have to hate it. You can just be neutral." Her web page is: www.marthacreek.com.

Another thought for readers to consider: My former wife discovered a study about the brains of people who died by suicide. A group of scientists in New York City did the study. She flew to New York and met with one or more of the scientists. The scientists concluded that the brains of victims of suicide all were similar and different from brains of people who died by other means. Many of us have suicidal thoughts at some point in our lives. The bottom line was the non-suicidal brains had a feature that convinced the person not to commit suicide. The brains of suicide victims had that part of their brain missing. I found that remarkably interesting. About three years after my former wife told me about the study, I was on an airplane flying to wherever and I sat next to a gentleman and we somehow started talking about suicide. Would you believe that this gentleman was one of the scientists who was part of the study? I told him what I learned from my former wife and he said that pretty much was what they concluded. I do believe there are no accidents. You may be thinking I'm not sure that I am a believer. OK I will give you another "no accidents" fact for you to think about. I attended a One Day University session in Sarasota, Florida on November 16, 2019. Each session has three speakers and one was from a university and she was an expert on our brains. Keep in mind that this was 25 years after Kim made her transition. After the workshop I talked to her and told her about Kim and the New York City scientific study on brains. I was pleased to learn that she was knowledgeable about the study and she agreed with the results.

I read the Daily Word every day. I will close by quoting a page out of the September October 2020 issue. The subject below is, "Forgive" Dated "Monday the September 21, 2020"

"Through forgiveness, I am free"

"When I seek to lighten the heaviness of my soul and heart, I consider what forgiveness work I may need to do to feel free. Forgiving does not mean condoning another's behavior or pretending it did not hurt. Rather it is a process to facilitate my healing and increase the lightness of my spirit.

Forgiveness does not have to involve seeing or speaking to the person I need to forgive. Perhaps that is possible only through a soul-to-soul silent exchange. I rely on divine love and wisdom in me to guide me through my forgiveness practice. Every step I take leads me to free myself of the weight I have been carrying. I go forward lighter and ever-ready to live more fully, refreshed, and invigorated."

The following bible verse for this issue is from "Ephesians 4:32"

"Be kind to one another, tenderhearted, forgiving one another, as God in Christ has forgiven you."

SOME OF THE BOOKS THAT HAVE HELPED ME IN MY LIFE JOURNEY, THEY MAY HELP YOU TOO

- Loving What Is by Byron Katie with Stephen Mitchell

- Question Your thinking, Change The World by Byron Katie

- I Need Your Love---Is That True by Byron Katie with Michael Katz

- A Mind At Home With Itself by Byron Katie with Stephen Mitchell

- When Bad Things Happen To Good People by Harold S. Kushner

- The Sermon on the Mount by Emmet Fox

- Daily Word by Unity Publications

- Lessons from the Light by George Anderson and Andrew Barone

WEB ADDRESSES THAT ARE HELPFUL

- Byron Katie's web address is www.thework.com

- Reverend Martha Creek's web address is www.marthacreek.com

JUDGE-YOUR-NEIGHBOR WORKSHEET

On the next page is Bryon Katie's worksheet that she has students complete prior to every one of her classes.

ABOUT THE AUTHOR

Julie Donnelly

Sometimes we may feel life is so hard that death is a great option. At 41 years old, I decided to take that route and God stepped in and prevented it. After screaming out for help, God lifted me up and a miracle happened to remove me from the situation. It started that same night by having me cry with a friend who later that evening told me that she learned about a need my company was having, requiring 5 people (out of 1500 possible respondents) to leave immediately for Honolulu, Hawaii. I applied that same night, and two days later was told I was chosen! In just 5 days my company sent me to Hawaii. While on a lonely beach in Hawaii two days later, shouting and crying about being abandoned, God spoke out loud to me! It not only saved me from that sad ending, it changed the direction of my life completely.

TEN

Finding God During the Darkest Days of My Life

By Julie Donnelly

Have you ever been in a position where you felt life was so terrible that you couldn't see a way out? Did you ever experience pain that is so deep it colors everything you do? In 1986, a lifetime of living in a dysfunctional home came to a head and I just wanted to stop the pain. We've all had difficult times in our lives, and who knows so much about another's pain that they can judge? Friends didn't know what goes on behind closed doors, yet many people did judge, adding pain to an already stressful situation.

I was living my dark night of the soul. I felt totally alone. I was Catholic at the time and I would go to church every day, praying for this situation to be lifted from my life. Finally, one day I couldn't take anymore, and I literally screamed out to God "Get me out of here!!!

And get me out of here RIGHT NOW!!! If you need to make me die, that's fine, but GET ME OUT OF HERE!!!"

Never judge someone who takes that sad option, you don't know what is going on in their mind. In my case I would be just fine, and then thoughts would flood my emotions. Suddenly I would head down that slippery slope and right before it was too late, I would see the crying faces of my two children, and I'd pull out of the inevitable.

My children saved my life. This was the first of multiple steps that God took to save me, but it wasn't until hindsight that I could see these steps.

I worked the 4PM-midnight shift in reservations for United Airlines at the time. I was on my way to work when I came so close to being "successful" that I was afraid to be alone anymore. On my way in to work I saw a good friend as she headed in toward the cafeteria. I was in a panic-state, so we sat while she listened and supported me. We both had off the next day, so she decided to give me a break and take me skiing for the day.

The "coincidence" of running into this particular friend was the next time that God worked to save my life. We had a briefing that we needed to read before work each day. My habit was to wait and read the briefing when I returned after my day off. My friend's habit was to read the next day's briefing before she left the office that night. This small difference changed my entire life! I didn't know it at the time, but it was also the next way God set things up to save my life.

At 11:50PM she came running over to me and told me to read the next days briefing. United had an emergency happening and they needed to send six reservations agents to Hawaii to help with the problem. There were 1500 eligible agents for just six positions! However, you needed to leave in just four days, and be gone from

December 15th to March 15th. I looked at it and said, "I can't do that, I have two kids, I can't leave during Christmas." Remember, I told God to "get me out of here NOW!" and God was setting it up for me.

My friend said , "Excuse me! Did you not try to take your own life today! Has this not become a habit! (not questions, she was stating facts). Yes, I said, it was true. She took my arms, looked into my eyes, and said "Julie, you will be dead by Christmas!" I agreed, sadly she was probably right.

United was telling everyone the next day while I was gone and having the selection on Friday – before I would have gotten back to the office. If not for my friend, I would have missed the opportunity to even be considered. God set up everything to make this particular friend be the first one I saw when I entered the office. I didn't know it at the time, but hindsight is 20/20.

I went to my supervisor's office and left a note on her desk asking her to put me in for consideration for this temporary transfer. As I put the note down, I said to God…" if you want me to stay here and sort all of this out, you won't let me get this. But, if you want me to move on in life, you'll let me get this transfer to Hawaii." (I still believed that God was "out there" someplace, I hadn't yet learned that God was in me.).

We went skiing the next morning and it was a wonderful day, filled with laughter! I didn't give a thought to Hawaii, or to my sorrows. In the future I would learn about the Law of Attraction and realize how important it was to let everything go.

The next day, Friday, I arrived at work at 3:30PM and my supervisor was standing there. I said to her "I didn't get it, right?" She said, "Yes you did, you leave on Monday morning!" I couldn't believe my ears! She repeated it again and I just started to laugh, cry, and do a little dance! God was working for me again, but I didn't understand that yet.

I won't go into everything that needed to happen in order for me to go. Imagine what you would need to go through if you found that in three days you were going to Hawaii for three months. The first thing was finding some money to go, and then to find a place to be when I got there. My supervisor helped with a temporary housing situation by calling on a favor from a friend in Hawaii. With that settled, my next task was to get some money. I called a friend to see about borrowing some cash, and fortunately she had some at home (our banks weren't open on Saturdays in 1986).

Everything was falling into place. I still didn't put God into this scenario, as to me God was still out there someplace, not involved with my day-to-day living. But it wouldn't be long before God became front and center in my mind.

Monday morning and I'm on my way to Newark airport. How exciting! I'd never been to Hawaii before, and I was heading for a three-month adventure. I didn't know even one person in the state of Hawaii, but I just looked at making new friends as a fun part of the adventure. And I was right!

Thirteen hours later I landed in Honolulu. I was beside myself with excitement! We drove past Waikiki Beach, Diamond Head, and the Honolulu Zoo. The smell of the flowers, the palm trees (remember, I was from New York, a great city without palm trees), and the Pacific Ocean right next to the highway. I was in heaven!

The next day I set off to explore the island of Oahu by bus. I didn't know that this was the day when I would find God. Not the God I knew as a Catholic, but the God I now know in Unity.

I got off the bus at a beach that I thought was called "the Pipeline," that is a famous area for surfers. I soon realized I got off at the wrong stop....or what I thought was the wrong stop! This beach was beautiful but the lava rock from ancient volcanoes came right up to the shoreline so there wasn't any swimming or surfing at this beach. The bus wouldn't return for an hour, so I decided to just sit on the beach and look at the water.

This is when my life took another major step to healing, and to finding God.

As I sat on the isolated beach, I started to think of my life, from birth until that moment. It was a painful journey. I had been a good Catholic. I did all the things I was taught would bring me blessings. I started to whisper…"where were you! I did my novena's, you weren't there!"

Then I was talking louder…"I said the rosary every day, you didn't listen! I wore a scapula, did the First Friday's, daily mass…you weren't there!"

Finally, I was marching up and down the beach, shouting out to the sky…" you are nothing! You are Santa Claus, the Easter Bunny… you don't even exist!" I picked up a handful of sand and threw it at "nothing." I crumbled to the sand and cried and cried until I couldn't cry anymore. How healing!

When I looked at it a few days later after finding God, I realized that I had to believe something was out there listening to me, or I was having a big fight with a cloud!

I finally stopped crying and got on the bus back to my new friend's home. That Sunday they woke me up to go to church because they figured with my name that I had to be a Catholic. I didn't want to insult them and say that everything they believe in is hogwash, so I got up and went to church. The priest gave a sermon that could only have been inspired by God. He said "this sermon has been given in every church, synagogue, mosque, and at meetings all over the world. Many of you have heard this sermon, but some of you need to hear it right now."

He proceeded to tell a story about a man in a house and the flood is coming. A rowboat arrives and tells the man to get in, but he says, "I've worn my scapula all my life, and I've gone to mass every day…. God will save me." Then the man was on the second floor and another rowboat came, but he said, "I've been saying novena's for years, and the rosary every day…God will save me." Next, he's on the roof and a helicopter came to get him but he said, "I've done my First Friday's… God will save me." And then the man drowned.

When he got to heaven he said to God "where were you! I did everything you told me to do and you didn't save me!" God said…" I sent you two rowboats and a helicopter, and you wouldn't get on!" By this time, I was crying again, I knew this sermon was meant for me!

After church I knew I had to find this beach again. I didn't know where I had gotten off the bus, so I was dependent on God telling me where to go…and of course, God did. I didn't know yet that God was inside me, always with me, but that understanding didn't come for a while yet.

Of course, I did get off the bus at the right stop. I sat on the beach and said "fine, what were my rowboats?" I closed my eyes and one by one there were years of situations appearing that would have changed my life and prevented what ultimately happened, but I had ignored them." After what felt like hours I said, "where was my helicopter?" and I heard a voice, as clear and loud as if someone was sitting next to me. The voice said, "you're on a beach in Hawaii aren't you!"

I started to cry happy tears because I realized that God had been with me the whole time! I rested in the fact that God is with me all the time, every day.

Hawaii was a real blessing. While I was there, I learned that God sees with my eyes, hears with my ears, tastes with my tongue, touches with my hands, and thinks with my mind. It was in Hawaii that I found Unity, and it was in Hawaii that I came to understand that God lives in me and through me.

ABOUT THE AUTHOR

Madelyn Balitz, LCSW, ACHP-SW

Madelyn Balitz is an author, speaker, and hospice professional with fifteen years of experience.

There are not many who have fulfilled so many intensely demanding roles, not only as a full-time social worker on hospice teams, but with her closest family members who had severe illnesses or accidents. She is one of those rare souls who transforms life's hardships into inspiration to others. She put her huge heart full of this inspiration into her recently published book, *All is Well: Understanding the End of Life, Caregiving, and Hospice Care.*

Madelyn serves on the Board at Unity of Sarasota.

ELEVEN

Solitude vs. Loneliness

By Madelyn Balitz

How comfortable do you feel about being your own best friend? Do you wish it were true, but it's not? Or are you clear that being with others is great, but being by yourself is just as wonderful, at least occasionally? Welcome to a journey from wretched loneliness to finding joy in one's own presence. I was thrust into this experiment when my husband died. I was writing a book at the time, doing everything "by myself" for the first time in my life, and struggling to make sense of it all.

In my 15 years of work as a hospice social worker, I had found plenty of ways to counsel people about loss and loneliness. I could speak to clients about their grief and loneliness with no discomfort, and I could see that this made a difference. But my own words were hollow and impotent as I faced this myself when my husband was diagnosed with terminal brain cancer and passed away just 10 months later.

It was inconceivable and seemed so *unnatural* for me to no longer be one of a couple. I had no idea how to consider who I was without doing so as defined by another person. One comes into the world alone and grows up to be an individual with unique qualities, thoughts, and identity. It's completely natural, but something else (being half of a deep and rewarding partnership) had come to feel natural to me. And then... the disruption of my natural day-to-day life was devastating.

But I could not allow myself to stay in that state for too long. I began experimenting with ways to get a grip, to remember who Madelyn was, to make peace with a broken best-friendship between me and myself.

If you can relate, know that you are not alone. During my last two years as a widow who still worked with hospice patients and their families every day, I've taken this inquiry to quite a deep level. One access road out of loneliness and into peace comes from reading the perspectives of others. For example:

"The reason that extended solitude seemed so hard to endure was not that we missed others but that we began to wonder if we ourselves were present, because for so long our existence depended upon the assurances from them." —Doris Grumback, award-winning author

My pain was the catalyst in this experiment. It moved me to research further this idea of solitude vs. loneliness and how I could speak the truth to help others. As I learned to access joy in solitude, I decided that my personal experience could be shared with others and I began to write this piece. I read many quotes that I found helpful that I wish to share with you and also give some insight to make them even more meaningful.

Like most every personal growth experience in life, it first takes an awareness and then the willingness to learn and change. Practice, practice, practice is the key to succeeding.

I ask that if you are struggling with this concept, take a deep breath and commit to an adventure with yourself, believing that this will be the most exciting and worthwhile experience that you could give to yourself. It has the potential of opening up so many doors and avenues for you. This journey is sure to build confidence, increase enjoyment, and has other pay-offs that are life-changing.

"Loneliness is the poverty of self; Solitude is the richness of self."
—Mary Sarton, American poet

How does one get to feeling so poorly of one's self? Does it start in our family of origin? Or in early years of schooling, from peers or adults? Wherever it starts, we are always able to begin anew, exploring and finding the rich and unique gifts within.

Even with faith that we have hidden riches within, how can we see these? We may start by asking a close family member or trusted friend to share what they see as unique or special about us. Sometimes we need that to get us looking more objectively at ourselves. It is helpful to write down at least one thing at the end of each day—how self expression showed up, or how we have impacted another person in a helpful or positive way. It's up to us to bring these to the forefront and acknowledge our unique qualities.

Solitude helps to find that inner, buried treasure. We must make time for quiet reflection and for self affirmation every day. As we rediscover what has been hidden, we can build on what is already true.

> *"Loneliness expresses the pain of being alone, and solitude expresses the glory of being alone."*
> —Paul Tillich, German-American philosopher and theologian

Have you ever felt extreme loneliness at the same time that you were with other people? When one is in a state of poverty of self, life is lonely, even in a crowd. The ache of loneliness can be soothed by reconnecting with yourself. It is *not true* that you have to be with others to not feel lonely, just as it *is true* that being with others doesn't always help. (When it does help is when another person helps you reconnect with yourself.)

For many who choose to stay home and raise a family, their roles as supportive wife and full-time mommy grow and grow while their sense of self shrinks. As one mom said, "I've nearly forgotten my first name. I'm only called 'hon' or 'mommy' all day and night. I pulled out my driver's license at the bank the other day and 'Susan' actually looked strange to me."

I notice that some people (whether in an "empty nest" due to children leaving, or because of divorce or the death of a spouse) look to the past to try and find themselves. One could go back to a previous career or rejoin a once-loved group like a tennis league. Others look to the future, going back to school to achieve a degree or finding a new volunteer opportunity, for example. However the search unfolds, it can open doors to reclaiming one's self.

One woman described this search as exciting and freeing; one told me it was scary and difficult. But each took that leap to find themselves all over again. The stronger that reconnection, the less one feels any ache of loneliness.

"I think it is very healthy to spend time alone. You need to know how to be alone and not defined by another person."
—Oscar Wilde

I spend an inordinate amount of time up close and personal with other people's families. As a liaison between a person in hospice care and their family, I get to know the dynamics, and, wow, I feel like "I've seen it all," though I'm sure I haven't.

Here is one dynamic I bet you have seen or experienced, too: A person can dramatically alter, depending on who they are with. A grown son speaks politely to me, then rudely snaps at his wife. A sobbing woman tells me about her relationship with her dying mother, but makes me promise not to say anything to anyone else in the family because they all think she's "as strong as an ox" and she would never want them to see her vulnerabilities.

I was conversing with a 50-year-old woman the other day whose father is in a nursing home with hospice care. The phone call was quite business-like, though pleasant enough. The next day, as agreed, I met her at the room of her father. Except then, she was *a different person*. Well, she was the same person, except an 8-year-old version! Her voice had changed into a quiet, little-girl tone when calling her father "Daddy." She literally asked him to "help me get through this." In other words, she was the small child, needing support and strength from her dad, instead of the competent adult visiting her dying father to offer comfort.

We can see that this is a dramatic example of "being defined" by someone other than yourself. But there are many subtle examples going on all the time. I'm not saying we have to talk and act exactly the same around everyone, but be aware of HOW you shift, with WHOM, and WHY.

The more you can notice this, the more you grow comfortable just being yourself.

The more you are comfortable being yourself, the more you will enjoy being with yourself, just in the company of your own thoughts and feelings.

And it is a self-reinforcing practice. When you spend more time getting to know your own thoughts, opinions, dreams, strong preferences, etc., the more you do not want to be defined by anyone else. You don't need that. You don't need the "benefit" of pleasing or appeasing another person, because you are fully in touch with the rewards of being comfortable with yourself. This is the most freeing thing you could ever do for yourself. As Wilde said, "You need to know how to be alone and not defined by another person."

> *"Solitude is the soul's holiday"*
> —Katrina Kenison

I love the idea of taking a holiday for the soul. To simply take time to just be and get back in touch with yourself. Like any holiday, it can require some planning, but be exciting to anticipate. For the soul's rejuvenation, it just means getting away from the world and all its problems and responsibilities in order to relax and be. *Being* is quite different than *doing*. As a friend of mine says, "Don't just do something, sit there!"

What a better way to give yourself a gift but then give your soul a holiday.

"Knowing how to be solitary is central to the art of loving. When we can be alone, we can be with others without using them as a means of escape"
—Anonymous

A client once told me of his fear of being alone and facing his own demons. To avoid that terror, he stayed very busy, a workaholic of sorts.

Now at the very end of his life, he shared that he regretted that he had not spent time with his family as he could have. And he said that now, when asked about his "last wishes," he was dismayed to realize that he had no idea…he had not ever spent time getting to know himself.

With help, he was able to verbalize his wishes and have some closure with his wife and sons. He advised them not to make the same mistakes, but to cherish all they were to themselves and those they loved every day. In ultimate sadness, he told them how sorry he was for all that he had missed out on in a lifetime with his family.

Do you think he could have had this profound realization earlier in life? If only he had stepped out of the rat race long enough to 1) think about what is important in life, and 2) feel his feelings and connect with his own heart.

"In solitude is healing. Speak to your soul. Listen to your heart. Sometimes in the absence of noise we find the answers."
—Dodinsky

As this man left this earth and transcended elsewhere, he left with a smile that let his family have peace. But they had regrets, too. There's nothing like death to awaken us to life, to the fact that here and now is our opportunity for connections with others, with one's self, and spiritually.

Especially during the COVID-19 pandemic, people had to deal with severe loneliness and the feeling of being disconnected from the world. I know I felt it, too. And yet, there was a gift in that—with the dramatic change in lifestyle and usual busy-bee-ness, there was more time to be with family at home and/or a lot more time to explore one's own needs, values, and priorities.

It was a time for many people to rekindle old loves such as painting or explore new interests such as writing a book. Those were the people who suffered with isolation and loneliness the least. The pandemic meant that we had to put a lot on hold and that pause gave rise to many epiphanies about what is truly important in life. Let's remember that we don't have to face imminent death like my client I described above, nor a crisis like the COVID-19 virus in order to find time to love ourselves and others.

"Being solitary is being alone well: being alone luxuriously immersed in doings of your own choice, aware of the fullness of your own presence rather than of the absence of others. Because solitude is an achievement."
—Alice Koller, PhD, author

In this quote we are invited to look at ourselves in the metaphoric mirror and ask, "Do I really like who I see?" If we do not see all the many levels of Self to appreciate, it would be hard to imagine enjoyment in being alone.

Many people were downright inspiring in the way they dealt with the COVID pandemic and all its repercussions. This showed me that no matter what the circumstance, there is an opportunity available for learning and growth.

"In solitude the mind gains strength and learns to lean upon itself."
—Laurence Sterne

Today's children seem to become easily bored and to always need a crutch to feel content—something like a video game. This is not an example of a solitary activity that fosters connecting with one's self. Remember what I wrote earlier about sometimes feeling the despair of loneliness even when with other people? It takes real connection with one's self or others for loneliness to lift. There was I time I remember when I too was bored but my parents or others were not the source of finding something to satisfy me. Often, I would take a bike ride to our small-town library and entertain myself for hours with stories skipping along through my imagination.

It is crucial to find ways to be in solitude which we don't just tolerate but come to appreciate and even look forward to. With consistent practice of solitude, loneliness loses its grip.

"There is a difference between loneliness and solitude, one will empty you and one will fill you. You have the power to choose."
—Ava, poet and author

A man I will call Ken was in need of my support as his wife in hospice care was nearing the end of her life. You have to remember, it's not only the end of her life, it meant the end of their marriage, the end of their travel adventures together, the end of their shared joy with their grandchildren, the end of Ken's life as he had known it.

Ken seemed very uncomfortable as we discussed some of the decisions before him. Embarrassed, he admitted that he really had not been tasked with any decision-making in his home or social life, that his wife had handled everything almost entirely for over 50 years. While having a "division of labor" is not uncommon in a marriage or partnership, this man had not *ever* looked to himself to make many important personal decisions. As he and I discussed this more, we decided that he may want to go home and take time in solitude to not dwell on his loss, but rather on what he has learned and gained from his wife's decisions over his lifetime with her.

He kept a journal of his thoughts and findings and came back to me with a surprise. During these moments of solitude, he said he had not felt lonely because he was too busy looking at his gains and gratitude's and how he planned to learn new things for him to survive on his own. He felt empowered and was willing to continue this writing exercise every day, so that he could go back and witness how he had grown and changed. He now had way to take charge of worry and fear around being lost without his wife.

Ken used the term "reborn" as he described how this exercise was affecting him. He said he knew he would always miss his wife, but that now he had solid ground to stand on, feeling stronger in himself than ever before.

> "...*Wherever we are, God is, and all is well...*"
> —Unity prayer

The sense that "all is well" is an attitude, something that we can take personal responsibility to generate, not a status report on everything outside of ourselves. The more we connect with and take care of ourselves, the more opportunity it gives others to do the same for themselves.

I am committed to continue to meet myself each and every day, and to acknowledge what I need to learn and what I have learned. Writing my book, *All is Well*, taught me more about myself than any endeavor I can recall. Maybe writing is your thing. To quote Lord Byron, "Letter writing is the only device for combining solitude with good company." Give writing every day a try, as that habit will always give you a bit of time to yourself.

I have found that giving loneliness its due time is necessary, but only its due time. As we have heard, it is not the number of years in your life that matter, it is the fullness of life in those years. Solitude can be life-expanding. Beyond enriching our own lives, the rewards of deep connectedness found in solitude can help others, maybe even contribute to a great change in the world. Start with a small step. What will you do today to quiet all the outside noise enough to hear your inner voice? Stop and listen, and answer. This is the doorway to gratitude and to enhancing your own life and lives of others. "Finding yourself" is always the first step.

"…Wherever we are, God is, and all is well…"

ABOUT THE AUTHOR

JULIE COOK DOWNING

Julie Cook Downing has a degree in Psychology plus Masters work in Industrial Relations and hired into management with AT&T from 1969-1985. Human Resources and Training was her professional path and in 1986, she became an Independent Consultant to Fortune 500 Companies with her expertise.

As a Unity member beginning in 1978 in Evanston, IL and Unity in Sarasota, FL beginning in 2001, she continues to serve multiple volunteer roles.

In 2000 she founded Caregivers' Comfort Creations®, LLC to Empower and Support Family Caregivers as an ongoing legacy to her Caregiving to her beloved parents.

TWELVE

The Greatest Gift to Us is Never Saying Goodbye

By Julie Cook Downing

It is my pleasure to welcome you to my personal transformation in the world of Family Caregiving where over 65 million of the U.S. population provides some type of Caregiving to their loved ones. YOU are either: A Current Caregiver, A Past Caregiver, A Future Caregiver or You Will Need a Caregiver.

If you are responsible for someone in your family that is not able to perform the routine daily living functions without help, you are a Caregiver! You may have parents or an elderly aunt living in another city, a child that is disabled living with you or in a facility, a sibling in another household, a close friend who is ill with no family or a wounded Veteran in the hospital recovering from being at war. Whether long-distance or not, if you have taken on the responsibility of that individual, YOU ARE A CAREGIVER.

Like almost ALL Caregivers, I did not know that I would become a family Caregiver in 1996 at the age of 48! Fortunately, following Spiritual Principles assisted me when my life became a life of such unexpected experiences. As you read my story, you will learn how my family life transformed.

Anyone who knew my family and me will tell you that as their only child, my parents, Katherine "Kitty" Cook and Culbreth "Cookie" Cook, loved and adored me and vice versa. If I exhaled, my parents inhaled and if I inhaled, they exhaled. One friend who went with me to visit my parents said that we treated each other as "deities". And my mother treated my dad with kid gloves as though he were a king; she was old school in being the consummate homemaker.

The three of us lived a fairy tale existence as a family and when I married my college sweetheart in 1970, we became a foursome fairy tale family long distance. My parents said there was no such word as son-in-law with Ted; he was their son.

As I look back, it was most unusual for parents to be as integrated into the lives of their adult children as my parents were in ours. In addition to my parents being fabulous human beings, all of our friends saw them as surrogate parents and/or grandparents to their children. Although my parents lived in Cleveland ,"Kitty and Cookie" or "Mama and Papa Cook" (the pet names our friends were encouraged to call my parents) were invited to attend the parties and celebrations of our Evanston friends where we lived. They attended anniversary, birthday, bar/bat mitzvah celebrations and many other good times. And any time Ted and I were celebrating, our parents made the trip to Evanston in addition to our annual memorable vacations together. Close friends our age who are like family, included my parents in some of the trips they invited Ted and me to take with them.

Living our married life in Evanston beginning in 1970 while my parents lived in Cleveland, meant that travel played a major role every time we got together. We usually saw each other every 3 months and my parents travelled to Evanston much more easily because my dad retired in 1976.

Our friends marveled at my parents because of their energy, zest for life and love of life. I, too, always admired these qualities in them among many other qualities. My dad had a doctorate and was an educator enjoying every day at the Community College where he retired as Assistant to the President.

When he turned 65, he continued to serve on many committees and boards and was even appointed to the Cleveland School Board. He was professionally active until he reached his 90th birthday.

My mother received her Masters in social work and worked for 9 years in top administration with the Girl Scouts before becoming a fulltime mother and housewife.

There was never anything that my parents and I disagreed on that created any issues or heartaches. During my teenage years, I was pretty normal in thinking that my parents did not know best for me when they refused to let me participate in fad dressing, ride in a car with dates before I was sixteen or date young men whose parents they didn't know. But these instances of misunderstanding lasted only moments. And into my adult years, there were no issues that I can even faintly recall that caused any sadness or discord among our family.

Along with their zest for life, they also had a very realistic outlook on death and dying. Their planning took the form of ensuring that their resources would care for them in good times and bad. As early as the 1980s, they put Advance Directives and Power of Attorney in place for me and Ted. Their personal affairs were organized in a manner that

I could put my hands-on information in an instant. Legal documents were kept up-to-date and I was personally introduced to all the players that would be a part of any contingency planning or arrangements. My parents even wrote an outline of pertinent facts for their obituaries. And because they believed in paying cash for ALL purchases, as generous as they were with me and my husband and our friends, they exquisitely planned and saved religiously in case of a rainy day.

The rainy day for our family began in the summer of 1995. My parents came to Chicago for the Presidential Inauguration of a dear friend into the National Medical Association. I observed that my mom was having trouble coordinating her outfits, was repeating herself and was not her outgoing self.

She was confused, not remembering from one moment to the next, and expressing concerns about her own health. The beginnings of severe disagreements visited our family and wreaked havoc among all four of us while we were together.

When my parents revisited for the Christmas holidays in 1995, there were more changes to my mom. She used to be Mrs. Santa Claus and had a talent for gift-giving along with being very creative. Ted, our friends and I loved receiving her gifts, but this Christmas was quite different. My mom was having trouble sorting gifts even with gift tags and I recognized that her mind wandered as she repeated herself much more.

During my parents' December 1995 visit, I told my dad that mom needed to see a neurologist while they were visiting. We secured an appointment in early 1996. My dad obliged and drove back to Cleveland to take care of business and returned for the appointment in time. The neurologist uttered the dreaded diagnosis of probable Alzheimer's disease.

Our lives were about to change dramatically. I had chosen not to become a parent because I'm sure that subconsciously I knew I could not be the role model to a child that my parents were to me. My life was already full and overflowing with a husband who loved me, parents who loved and adored me, friends who were like family plus the numerous pets who could claim being part of our family. I was so grateful for the love surrounding me that I never thought I would become a parent to my parents.

The MOST disagreeable time was to last for approximately three years and those years actually became the ultimate gift to me. Even during my mother's illness and subsequent death, I can look back at these trying times and credit my mother with being her same giving and angelic self by offering me the opportunity to help others by blending my professional passion for Human Resources with Family Caregiving and my spiritual connection.

My entire professional life has revolved around people issues: my degree is in psychology with Masters studies in Industrial Relations. For 17 years I was in management in Human Resources and Training within the multi-billion-dollar telecommunications industry of AT&T. In 1986, I started my own business as a Human Resources Consultant specializing in Training and Development. My clients included Ameritech/AT&T, National Easter Seal Society, Baxter Healthcare, ICI Pharmaceuticals, Federal Reserve Bank, Kraft, and Northern Trust to name a few. I have also had the privilege of a being a presenter at national conventions of the Society for Human Resource Management.

In addition to being a Human Resources professional, I am also an entrepreneur and have enjoyed a myriad of business activities. I co-launched a popcorn company in Chicago that served Nieman-Marcus, developed a coupon book for fitness and health-related products that was promoted on ABC and sold at Marshall Field's and coordinated a Minority and Women In Business video utilized by Ameritech throughout their Midwest Region featuring actress Mariette Hartley. There have been no consulting or entrepreneurial challenges to date that have equaled the Caregiving role that I embarked upon. And there have been no activities in advance that adequately prepared me for my Caregiving role. Knowing that God is in charge certainly helped to support me.

At the same time, I became a long-distance Caregiver to my parents at age 48, my dad at 84 became a primary Caregiver to my mom at age 79, and for the first time in his 55 years of married life, he became responsible for all of the activities my mom had orchestrated during their entire marriage. These activities included managing the home, arranging meals, handling finances, responding to/and organizing any social interactions and countless other activities. What a change for our family! And what a dramatic change I witnessed in our family dynamics as my dad assumed more and more Caregiving responsibilities while at the same time being in denial about my mom's condition which is often the norm for Caregivers dealing with Alzheimer's.

DAD

Dad put up a good front of covering for my mom, but he was unable to hide her diminished mental state. For the first time in my 48 years, my dad and I disagreed. My parents owned their 14-room home with 4 floors for 49 years, and I knew my dad needed help in the home NOW. My dad was adamant that after all the kid glove care he had received from my mom; it was his turn to take care of her. But he really did not have a clue about what to do, so we argued about the way things should be and I spent a tremendous amount of time setting up help… only for my dad to dissolve it. Our roles changed dramatically, and I truly became the parent.

Ted and I were long-distance Caregivers to both of my parents while they remained in their home from 1996 to 1999, and for about one and a half years of those agonizing three years, I was unsuccessful in getting my dad to accept the kind of concentrated outside help that he needed. There were times when my husband actually feared that my dad could suffer a heart attack due to the arguments we had because of dad's insistence on solo Caregiving. For the first time in his life, my dad experienced high blood pressure and I mean HIGH – over 200! He believed that he was capable, even in his mid-eighties, of handling any and all situations that could arise from Caregiving experiences.

One and a half years into his Caregiving, my dad finally agreed to have a 7-day weekly paid Caregiver for my mom and accepted hiring the professional Care Manager in Cleveland that I approved. During our family's experience with my mom's evolving dementia, I realized that I had been given a new direction in life by recognizing the need for tools to assist, support and motivate Caregivers beyond the support group I attended and the Care Manager I hired. I saw the dramatic metamorphosis take place in my dad both physically and emotionally as he embarked upon his Caregiving role.

As a volunteer in the Caregiving programs in my Unity on the North Shore church in Evanston, I began integrating my professional and volunteering skills into my new life as a Caregiver and reflecting on the many positives in my Caregiving role. In spite of all the pluses in my Caregiving life due to my parents' expert planning, it was with great introspection that I also monitored my own emotional state: so many frustrations, so much sadness and pain, so many helpless feelings, and so much bewilderment that my parents, who were so perfect, so smart and so immortal, had become imperfect in the wake of illness and Caregiving issues. I was brought up believing that humans are 99% spiritual and only 1% human in the event they transitioned.

Observing my dad's primary Caregiving role still in the home and assisting in my own Caregiving experiences both long distance and during frequent visits to Cleveland, taught me the extraordinary values of: organization, recording data, noting doctor's visits, recording patient observations, listing telephone numbers and even taking time out to write my own thoughts. It was also important to me to reinforce a daughter's appreciation to my dad for not jumping ship (he was a Navy man) even though we could not agree on Caregiving methodologies.

I decided to create a 366 Day Journal and Record for my dad that would express my appreciation and provide a means of organizing data for the Caregiving taking place in our household. My dad called it the "book of the millennium" and was deeply touched beyond any words. When he received the professionally designed and color-printed book copyrighted in 2001, he was speechless. Beginning in 2013, I created my Caregivers' Comfort® Inspirational Planning Caregivers and Veterans' Caregivers Calendars with some of my Journal patterning.

With my parenting, my dad finally moved from the extreme of not wanting help, to selling and exiting their home. In February of 1999 we placed my mom into Cleveland's top Retirement residence in the Alzheimer's unit and dad moved into Independent Living in the same Residence. We continued to be blessed and recognize God's presence with dad paying $10,000 monthly.

My mom only lived until July, 1999, 6 months after her move. She fell and broke her hip and that was the beginning of the end. So many with Alzheimer's disease will live in a vegetative state for years and years and years. She lasted only 3 years with Alzheimer's disease. Our "family" friend, Rev. Pat Williamson, former Chairman of Unity World Headquarters and our former minister of Unity on the North Shore in Evanston, came to Cleveland to be the Minister for my mom's Celebration. A Path to Spiritual Awakenings for me was additionally provided with this Celebration.

After my mom's death, I became a long-distance Caregiver to my dad. He enjoyed independent life in his large Independent Living apartment for 2 years and then my regular commutes to Cleveland confirmed his diminished mental capacity as a result of several strokes. He was our family historian and all of a sudden he could not remember events. His mind became perfectly blank so I moved him from Independent Living to Assisted Living in Cleveland.

Simultaneously, I became my husband's Caregiver who needed back surgery because of a bulging disc that prevented him from walking. A year after his successful surgery, we decided to relocate in December 2001 to warm Sarasota, FL where we vacationed annually beginning in 1981. My husband suggested that we bring my dad from Cleveland to live with us because commuting between Florida and Ohio would be very cumbersome.

My dad and I were joined at the hip and experienced camaraderie that meant the world to both of us. The saddest time in my entire life was having my dad live with us.

©Style Magazine 2005 by Ruth Lando/Photo by Alex Stafford

I found my mother's and father's mental demises "the saddest thing in my entire life. It tugs at every fiber of my being."

Being in charge of his daily existence and seeing his diminished state every day was so depressing for me. My dad was financially self-sufficient so I hired 7-day a week Caregivers to come to our home because the responsibility and sadness were overwhelming to me. This was the man who loved me, protected me and lived for every breath I drew. And now he was dependent on Ted and me 24/7. As diminished as he was, it was still so evident to me and all who knew us how much he loved me. Life transforms but true relationships continue.

Dad died of a massive stroke in February 2006. Both Ted and I believe that bringing him to Florida extended his life and he called me "his girl" up until the very end.

And our "family" friend, Rev. Pat Williamson, returned to Evanston to minister the Celebration of my dad. Again, true reinforcement of Universal Spiritual Principles in Celebration of my dad.

I never thought I'd be a parent to my parents, but I am proud of my contributions to the parents who nurtured and treasured me as long as they could and stayed with me after they transitioned. It hit me really hard that if I was experiencing such emotional trauma and I had ALL POSITIVES in my relationship with my parents and my Caregiving situations, what must others be experiencing with SO MANY NEGATIVES? Those "others" being: people who have never had a loving relationship with family members requiring Caregiving OR whose family members didn't or couldn't provide the financial resources to provide adequate care and/or respite from Caregiving responsibilities OR who don't have credible healthcare provisions OR have siblings and other family members that won't carry their equal Caregiving responsibilities and on and on and on.

My Caregiving Blessings led me to found Caregivers' Comfort Creations ®, LLC in 2000, a company dedicated to Empowering and Supporting Caregivers throughout the country. My company is a daily legacy to my parents and is MY best example of NEVER SAYING GOODBYE TO OUR LOVED ONES.

ABOUT THE AUTHOR

Kaileia (KyKye) Kostroun

Kaileia (KyKye) Kostroun is an intuitive writer of poetry, literary fiction, and creative non-fiction. She is working towards her BFA in Creative Writing from Ringling College of Art and Design in Sarasota, Florida. Notable publications include: "Salacia" in SCENE Sarasota Magazine, "Eclipsed" in Mookychick Magazine, and articles for TheTravelIntel.com. She is also a Thespian alumni and graduated Theatre major from the Academy for Performing Arts in Scotch Plains, New Jersey. Kaileia's mission is to cradle human hearts with her words. Connect with her on Instagram @_eclectickye and @kaileiawrites.

THIRTEEN

The Mermaid's Emergence

By Kaileia Kostroun

I'm searching for my reflection in the bathroom mirror, but I don't see me.

I see my brother dressed in beige, behind a thick, glass window in a tiny stall. My mom and I wait in line for hours to see him for only a few minutes. He moves in and out of rehabilitation centers, county jail cells, and halfway houses for eight years. He misses holidays, birthdays, graduations, and vacations.

Drug Court's zero tolerance policy doesn't distinguish between six nanograms of marijuana or a full-blown heroin relapse. They sentence him to state prison because that's how the system grants justice to those who suffer from addiction.

I come home from school one afternoon and walk past his empty bedroom for the third day in a row. All of his clothes are still there but his life force energy feels distant.

My mom is seated at the kitchen table. "Where's Alex?" I ask her.

Puddles form in her puffy eyes and that's when I know.

My mom's tears over the years permanently stain the walls of my heart. I don't think it hurts my younger sisters in quite the same way. They don't get a chance to know him, the real him, beneath the pain he numbs. Soon, all he ever shows anyone is the darkness to which he succumbs.

I learn to grieve the loss of someone who is still alive. At one point, he is so far gone, I can't recognize him in his own eyes.

Mom always asks me, "Don't you see his eyes? Can't you tell he's on something?"

I teach myself not to, so I can have my brother back. He's here. He's here because I want him to be here.

When I finish staring at the stranger in the bathroom mirror, I wash my face, dry my eyes, and practice smiling before I join Jacen in his room. I can't control my emotional flashbacks or their intensity, and my boyfriend never understands why he's a trigger.

I lie down next to him and examine his eyes. A mesmerizing blend of green and blue, and pale red. His breath reeks of alcohol and smoke. I pretend it doesn't.

I hope he doesn't fall asleep early again. Leave me there awake to drown in my emotions. I think back to promises he's made and attempt to count how many are still full. I look for reasons to stay.

"I want to talk to you," I say, attempting to steal his eyes away from the television screen.

"Okay, so talk."

If only it could be that simple. Fish a single thought from the stream rushing through my brain. I am silent for too long, so he says something instead.

"Nothing in life matters."

"Nothing matters?"

"Nope. None of this means anything. You don't matter. I don't matter. It's a miracle we're even here."

"It *is* a miracle. Wait, so this, us, means nothing to you?"

"No. You mean everything to me."

"But you just said—"

"Exactly, so it means even more since nothing matters."

Nothing he says tonight speaks to my soul, just chews away at it. We go back and forth until he gets tired and passes out. I can't help but feel alone even when we're together.

I stare at the red numbers on the alarm clock while darkness caresses my skin with a cold, empty temptation. My stomach aches. Saliva pours from my cheeks and fills my mouth. I swallow and pray the nausea goes away by morning.

When I arrive home, I can barely breathe. My chest is tight, as if my heart sank and my stomach swallowed it. I still have no appetite, but Zen invites me to join her and Kent for lunch.

Zen and I live together. Her hair is a lion's mane of brown curls— wild as she is. She is fierce yet gentle, my Gemini twin. I feel at ease in her presence, like coming home.

We arrive at Kent's apartment building and he is already waiting out front. Even at 70 years old, his inner child shines through when he smiles. His eyes are intense, but they soften as they meet ours. Kent says his mission in life is to empower women because women were kind to him throughout his entire life.

He informs us about the vagus nerve— how information enters through the gut, goes up through the brain, and finally, makes its way down into the heart, because all wisdom lies in the heart.

"Your gut is a castle. You need a guard to filter who or what comes in."

The message doesn't come from him. It comes through him.

Zen and Kent bounce questions, ideas, and revelations off one another. I listen intently, observing every gesture with a sense of awe and wonder.

Zen holds my hand in hers. She knows I have a hard time speaking up and remembering that I am not a passive passenger in my story; I am an active participant. I smile at her, comforted by her touch, her effortless understanding.

After lunch, we walk to the Bayfront park, a magical place where each tree is a character with its own personality. Zen and I slip off our shoes and tip toe over jagged rocks to dip them in the water.

"Oh my god," Kent says, eyes wide on me. "She's a mermaid. Look, she's emerging from the water."

Kent's ADHD kicks in full force. He begins referencing classic literature, switching between *The Odyssey* and *Frankenstein*.

"Make the monster beautiful."

"Sirens are the daughters of memory."

Memories. They flow through me, dragging me back to places I've been, cycling waves of familiar emotions.

"Can sirens be heard on land too?" I ask him.

"You're the mermaid. You tell me."

"Well, I'm asking because I feel like I can hear them. But I don't know."

"Don't say you don't know. If you feel it, then that's your truth."

"Wow, why can't other people see me this clearly?"

"Because they don't understand the water. You can only connect with people who do because that is your element. You're not an earth creature."

"We're not from here either," Zen adds. Her eyes light up as she laughs. "Kent, where did you come from?"

"You and I were flying around in a spaceship. And then somehow, we crashed. Wait, who was driving?"

"You were driving. That's why we crashed."

"Oh god, you're right!"

The three of us are present in each moment whenever we are together. No drugs, no alcohol. Yet we are so high.

Kent tells me I am a golden-eyed unicorn and thanks me for listening to him, for reflecting his words back to him so he can learn from himself. Zen says almost the same thing; I really listen when someone is speaking; I absorb it and take it to heart.

But my boyfriend is right. Our strengths can become weaknesses. That is what happens the day I agree to meet up with a stranger in a hotel room.

A man reaches out to me online, claiming that in exchange for companionship, he can provide a generous weekly allowance. I email his former sugar baby since he provides me with a reference. I think it odd he even has a reference, but I keep an open mind. She has nothing but kind words to say about him. According to her, he respected her time and always made her feel comfortable. Thanks to him, she is graduating from law school debt free.

I reflect on my first sugar dating experience: I meet a man for dinner and go back to his house for tea. He shares his entire business philosophy with me because he knows I'm actively listening and engaged in the conversation. But it's getting late, so I get up to leave. He pecks me on the lips goodbye, stuffing a couple hundred dollars in my purse as thank you.

But I can already tell, this is not the kind of man I am about to meet.

This man contacts me after I tell him I am not available to call, email, or chat. When I finally pick up the phone, he says he wants to meet as soon as possible to discuss the terms of a potential arrangement. I have a whole two-and-a-half-hour drive to think it over, to turn around, to call him back and tell him, *No, I don't want to see you.* But I don't. I keep driving.

He calls me repeatedly, wanting to know how far I am.

It's pouring rain. The sky is warning me, *Don't go!* but I don't listen. I don't listen to myself or the sky. I just keep driving.

But why, you ask?

Because my mom has cancer and is charging her medical bills on a credit card. Because my dad has been furloughed. Because my college raised their tuition bill and we still haven't figured out a way to pay for this upcoming semester. Because I receive an email from my landlord stating my lease is non-renewable, so now I need to find a new place to rent that I can afford, and fast. Because I feel guilty. Because I can't do anything, so I'm trying to do something.

Expressionless, I walk to the door. Unsurprisingly, he calls again.

"Meet me in my room, on the first floor, at the end of the hall."

"Okay, I'm here," I tell him.

But I'm not here. I'm not in my body. I'm in my mind. But my mind isn't clear. My mind is cloudy like the sky.

Once I walk through the door, I know there is no turning back. This man is over 200 pounds. He is six feet, two inches tall and wears a gold chain around his neck. I take off my clothes when he tells me to. I do as he says. I listen, even though what I really want to do is speak.

It is as if I am observing myself from an outer perspective. I forget I am an active participant in my own story. I fall into the role of the passive passenger again, the observer, the peacemaker. I keep the peace.

I do as I am told to avoid confrontation. And in a few minutes, it's over. I put my clothes back on. We leave the room and walk out of the hotel through the side door. He turns the corner.

And I never see him or hear from him again.

After I'm home, I re-read the email exchange with his former sugar baby. My nausea returns with a vengeance. I realize there is a good chance his reference was actually an alias.

He scammed me. Not that it matters now, to anything other than my pride. My fragile 20-year-old body cannot process it yet, like the aftershock of a gaping wound. Painless, until you notice there's blood.

I don't care about the money. I don't care about anything. I don't even cry. I am just grateful to be alive. It could have been so much worse.

I keep thinking about things my boyfriend said. "The problem is you're too trusting. You don't see things how they really are. Not everyone means well or has good intentions. People will do whatever they can to survive. At the end of the day, you just have to act like everybody wants something from you."

I don't want any of it to be true. That is not the lens I want to see the world through.

It takes me two days before I can finally admit to myself that it did actually happen, that I was naive enough to let it happen. I decide to take the necessary steps and precautionary measures to reclaim my power, starting with my physical body and emotional health.

I am redirected by various medical staff. As I speak to them about my situation, I feel shame rise in my stomach and fall from my eyes in the form of tears. I am laying in a hospital bed in the ER while specially trained nurses reassure me that what happened was not my fault, that I had good intentions. But I know what I did. Nothing. I didn't do anything. And I could have. After 6 hours, I am free to leave. They gift me a soft purple blanket to take home. I feel taken care of. Baby-steps.

This is not something I feel comfortable sharing with my family. I am done acting out of obligation because I've seen where it leads. They don't need the added stress. Neither do I.

This *is* something I feel like I need to share with my closest friends. And my boyfriend.

"I tried to tell you how people are, how this world is," he starts, enraged. "Why didn't you listen to me?"

"I'm sorry. I didn't think that would happen. If I knew, I wouldn't have gone."

"What else did you think would happen? Geez, I can't even look at you."

"Jacen, please. Can you just listen to me? Can you hear me out?"

"You went behind my back."

"I'm not the only one," I snap.

"That's completely different."

"Why? Because it's you? Don't act like things have always been perfect between us. Trust was already an issue. We aren't even officially back together."

"Well I thought we were more."

"We are."

"Apparently not."

He drinks until his pain can no longer be contained. I cry through mine, and his. I try to explain myself but there is nothing to say. Why didn't I confide in him before it was too late? I drove right past his exit. The answer is as simple as it is sad; I didn't believe I could.

"Tell me what his name was! Tell me where I can find him."

"I already told you, I don't know."

I'm even more embarrassed now that the whole neighborhood can hear us. His mom steps in and serves as the much-needed mediator. She listens to me. She helps me speak up despite his growing rage.

"Stop screaming at her!" she says. "You're taking her power away again."

He glares at me, brows furrowed.

"Do you love her?" she asks him.

"Of course, I do," he admits. "More than anything."

"Then you need to be there for her. Right now, she doesn't need to be screamed at. She needs you to be there for her. You two are a team."

"I need to kill this guy first."

"Did you ask her if that's what she needs? If that will help her?"

"It'll help me."

"Ask her."

He turns to me, reluctantly. "Would it?"

I shake my head. "It won't. It doesn't change what happened. Besides, if you kill him, then it's your win. Not mine."

"Let her have her win, Jacen."

I feel the urge to speak. I don't care if he's listening, but I need to say my truth out loud, for me.

"I take responsibility for the part I played in all of this. Ignorance is not innocence. I just hate feeling like I can never feel my lows because I have to stay high for you when you're low— even now, when I'm at my lowest. When you're drunk or high and we're together, I get these intense emotional flashbacks and suddenly, I'm reliving what I went through with my brother all over again. It makes me feel alone, like there's this unbreakable wall between us and I can't fully connect with you the way I want us to. How are we supposed to build trust together when I don't even feel confident that you're really here?"

They both wrap their arms around me. They told me I was loved and supported before, but I actually believe them this time. The Universe continues to show me that it is okay to lean on others. I am not heavy. I am light. And when my boyfriend holds me through the following nights when I can't sleep, he finally says the words I've been craving to hear for over a year, "I got you. I'm right here."

Sunrise walks help me get back into my body and out of my head. I let people love me in the best way they know how. I accept help and care. And I realize how alike we humans all are.

Then I receive a call from the police department. An officer asks me to relive the most nauseating experience of my life just so he can tell me, "You didn't say no. You didn't tell him to stop. You showed up. What did you honestly expect? Lying is not against the law."

It's over. Case closed. In the law's eyes, my brother is a criminal and I am a prostitute.

Sitting on the beach, every pudgy old man who walks by triggers a flashback. I write a poem for each wave of emotion as it crashes. I let them flow. I let them go. I allow them to come again, if they need, until I am finally at peace.

I take my time getting into the water, no longer feeling the need to look around and see who might be watching. I surrender to the flow, trusting the ocean to carry me. The water feels safe.

Floating on the waves with eyes closed, I can no longer feel the skin that separates my body of water from the body of water I'm in. Every part of me melts back into the whole, where all of me always belongs. I remember my true nature— my inner mermaid. I may have lost my crown in the sand, but I own this throne here in the water. I am still royal.

In life, there is no clear beginning, middle, or end. Life, like the waves, is cyclical. The water we are made of is ever flowing. And all that we think, feel, and know eventually washes away, over and over again. Each time, different shells remain containing an imprint of a lifeform that once called it home. But through it all, what we keep until we can no longer be kept, is our memories. Only then are we truly free. For now, we have the choice to stay silent, or to speak and move freely from our hearts. When my heart speaks, my fingers listen. And if my mouth can't say the words aloud, the truth can always be read in my eyes, or on the page.

ABOUT THE AUTHOR

Susan Parry

Susan was born and raised in Erie, Pennsylvania and has dabbled in writing all her life, both professionally and personally. After a liberal arts college education, she began a career in corporate communications, followed by freelancing, then positions in early childhood education, computer science, a nanny for several families, and finally as a pet sitter. The latter allows more time for writing, which is her first love as well as her major frustration! In her free time, she volunteers as a Friend of the Library, as a National Public Radio supporter, and as an environmentalist in many areas of involvement and support.

FOURTEEN

My Inspiration

By Susan Perry

"Life is all in how you look at it"

I buy a lot of greeting cards for family and friends, and many years ago found one I thought particularly appropriate for my friend Amy. It shows a frog having trouble hopping lily pads while another frog provides encouragement from the pond's edge. The hopping frog finally makes it, and the card's caption reads: "Thanks for being there."

I first remember Amy when we were teenagers growing up in the 1950's. We were at a mutual friend's slumber party, and the highlight of the evening was trying to get our hostess to say a particular swear word that in those days never crossed a "nice" girl's lips.

Finally, we succeeded, but throughout our relentless efforts, Amy kind of held back. I thought maybe she just didn't know how to have fun like the rest of us, and for a time I viewed her as a "goody-goody."

I mean, this kid respected every rule her parents set down and she not only worked, she even saved her money? And she never complained about a thing. To boot, she was as cute and flawless as Debbie Reynolds and had a very handsome boyfriend. By contrast, I was making weekly trips to a dermatologist and squeezing into a size 14!

Except for occasional parties, I didn't see much of Amy until the spring of 1962 when we finally had some things in common.

We had both quit college and were living at home. And we both had jobs as salesclerks in local clothing stores. Our friends were still in school, so by default, we befriended each other.

Amy had tremendous faith and practiced it regularly. She was a church goer, and I was not, but that summer I let her cheerfully rouse me from many a Sunday sleep-in to attend sunrise services at a local drive-in.

There she'd be at pre-dawn, all fresh and chatty, to whisk me off for a little religion. As my resistance wore down, her enthusiasm proved infectious, and by the time church was over, I found I felt as good as she did. After that year, we grew apart through her marriage and my relocation to another city.

I happened to be back home when her father died but didn't go to either the funeral home or to the funeral. This hurt Amy deeply, and she let me know it.

Her gentle explanation of needing me to be there for her at such a time came as a startling revelation to me. I had never experienced a loved one's death, nor did I have enough confidence in myself to think I could be consoling or supportive. It was through this experience that I began to understand that friendship carries certain responsibilities, and now I make sure I'm there at such times.

Amy has taught me much more as well. When I was already divorced and struggling financially and emotionally as a single parent, Amy was waging a losing battle to keep her own marriage intact.

No matter how miserable the situation, with Amy the show always went on, and this was especially evident each Christmas when she invited scores of her "stray" friends out to the family cabin to cut our own Christmas trees. Such traditions were her emotional glue, and I greatly admired her ability to stay focused on the good.

Amy also had an uncanny knack for seeing the humor and forgiveness in all things. Like the time I inadvertently donated my father's brand-new winter coat to a local charity.

When I realized what I had done, I called Amy in a panic. Her immediate response was to have me pause, catch my breath, and enjoy visualizing the person who probably now had the coat. Did he or she have shoes? Did the coat double as a blanket? Did my mistake possibly bring a smile to someone who hadn't smiled in a long time? This lightness on her part lightened me, and although my father was not happy about my seeming carelessness, I no longer beat myself up for making mistakes.

Hugs from Amy are legion. Arms always outstretched in greeting to envelop you in joy sorrow, or anything in between. Until her influence, I considered hugging as pretty much a family-only gesture, and infrequent at that. Now I hug others freely and value such touching as an invaluable way of connecting in a culture that all too often fosters isolation.

Amy and I have lived far apart for over 30 years, she in Florida and me in Pennsylvania, but the glue in our friendship never weakens. It's as though she's always with me. If I'm having a bad day, she magically calls. Or a surprise might arrive in the mail; something I forget I've ever mentioned wanting.

I have saved letters from Amy dating back to the mid 1980's, and it turns out she was saving mine because one day out of the blue, a packet of them arrived in the mail. These missives are invaluable to me for seeing where we've been and how far we've come in our respective lives. Amy's letters were full of family news, updates on her spiritual journey, and always included encouragement and suggestions about how to handle whatever personal dilemma I was dealing with at the time.

In one such letter, out fell a check for $150.00! I was dumbstruck. This was in 1990 when I was juggling a return to college with a full-time job and licking my wounds over the end of a supposed "forever" relationship. Mounting financial worries added to the mix. Here is Amy's explanation of the check:

... "My mother had given me some money…and I felt flush. I needed to give to my spiritual source…and I was feeling a real strong bond with you. Please accept this and know that we call it windfall money. That means that it can only be used for something that is fun and special that we wouldn't ordinarily be able to do or buy. You don't even have to tell me what you decide to do. Just enjoy and know that you are very special to me."

Turns out, this windfall came just in the nick of time for me to afford splitting the bill with friends for a birthday dinner at an upscale restaurant, which I had been about to decline due to financial constraints!

Other letters from Amy share lessons learned, particularly one Christmas in 1984 when circumstances precluded spending the holiday as she always had. In her words:

"I realized that as long as everything was going to be different, then I wasn't going to try to make anything the same as it had been in the past. If it was going to be different, then the whole day would be different, no plans, just wing it…Needless to say, it was perfect…We are all changing, and our habits must change too. I don't want to be sad because I tried to make things the same and it didn't work. I am changing and I like it."

In many ways, Amy's letters have also been an advice column. I would pour out my problems to her and back would come a very direct response to my laments. Following is an excerpt from one of my favorites regarding proper behavior with men both at home and while on my business trips.

"There is no reason in the world why you can't go into the bar for a drink after dinner. We have come to a point that women are allowed to do that without everyone (except our mothers) thinking the worst. That is the great thing about being out of town. Who is going to tell them? You have good judgment and good taste. Trust your own instincts. Remember the appearance you give off makes it very clear that you are a sophisticated lady who is very choosy. It is alright to have male friends and go out to have fun and a free meal without going to bed with them. That can be made very clear to begin with so there aren't any surprises. I have a friend here who is in much the same situation…She is in sales, so she goes to a lot of businesses. She gets asked out for a drink and she goes. She doesn't even drink. She also always meets them somewhere. They never come to her house and she never goes to theirs, until she really knows them. You set your own guidelines and stay in them, and I know that you can have fun and feel good about yourself too. I am sure that you know all this anyway. I have never been in your situation so I really shouldn't give advice. I guess that what I have said is the way I wish I would feel if I were in your shoes…Keep that chin up and know that you are one fantastic lady who deserves the very best. There are lots of nice men out there you can keep company with, and who knows, one of them might turn out to be Mr. Right. We don't have to know it right away!"

Amy's spiritual journey continued well beyond the sunrise drive-in church services with me in our youth. She was looking for the right church to call home, and while still living in Erie, discovered Unity, which fit her beliefs beautifully. Soon she was corralling me and others to join her in a Mastermind Group, in which we applied Unity principles through use of a daily journal system to guide us toward living the life we desired. We met weekly, and for me, this was a lifeline at a time when much in my personal life was unraveling. Our group disbanded when Amy moved to Florida in 1990, but for several years after, she gifted me the journal as she knew how much it helped me stay focused on the positive.

In Florida, Amy soon joined a Unity church, becoming a devoted parishioner and volunteer. The more involved she became, the more she wanted to expand her spiritual growth and decided to attend classes at Unity Village near Kansas City, Missouri, the world headquarters of the Unity church. There, she flourished in her studies and managed to return several times for additional courses. By then she had become an assistant to the reverend at her home church and felt a strong calling to become a Unity minister. With encouragement from her church, her family and many friends, Amy applied, was accepted, and began Unity Ministerial School in 1996. She was ordained in 1998.

Amy loves to celebrate birthdays, including her own, and never hesitates to remind others when hers is approaching. One birthday of note came on the heels of her having lost someone special in her life due to a freak accident. When she returned to Florida from the services and burial in Pennsylvania, her Unity "family" and friends had a surprise birthday party at her house. Amy describes it in one of her letters to me:

"There were at least 40 people…the cake was the biggest cake I have ever seen. There was a church on one side…On the other side was an angel with a trumpet. The angel had 'Amy' underneath. The cake said, 'happy birthday to our special angel.' Sharon, who is black, went with her boyfriend (also black) to order the cake. The angel was a brown angel. Isn't that wonderful?"

This year, 2020, on August 5, Amy celebrated her 80th birthday, and that is part and parcel of why this is a perfect time to honor her with my essay. She has meant so much in my life, nudging me along to clear many personal hurdles and to believe that anything is possible.

Since ordination as a Unity minister in 1998, Amy has served several congregations in Florida, and most recently serves as Associate Minister & Volunteer Coordinator with Unity of Sarasota. I visited her there in 2016 and could plainly see that this is where she belonged…a true 'meant to be' for my longtime friend who knew her spiritual calling from the time she was a kid.

ABOUT THE AUTHOR

Lisa Arundale

Lisa Arundale is originally from Virginia. Lisa has sung for audiences since childhood. She composed & performed campaign songs to help pay her way through college. Her audiences have included Elizabeth Taylor, Robert Guillaume, Clint Eastwood, two US Presidents, Governors & US House Representatives.

Lisa opened for Wayne Dyer at the Van Wezel sponsored by Unity of Sarasota and currently sings jazz standards with "The Stardust Memories Big Band" in Naples.

Owner/CEO of a corporate training/consulting company, she lived in 5 states & traveled to 49. Lisa and Dwight lived in Boca Grande, FL and Martha's Vineyard, MA. Lisa recently moved to Sarasota.

FIFTEEN

Leaning Into Grief – The First Year

By Lisa Arundale

Grief
Grief, you wash over me like the ocean waves
break across a sandy beach,
disrupting the shell of calm I have created.
I pensively court the knowing that you will pounce upon me
again and again, stirring my soul with each visit,
rendering me helpless against my sorrow,
forcing me to take an inventory and build the shell again
with whatever you have left me.

Grief, I fear you are here to destroy me, Until…
after many visits, I realize the sands that make up my soul
are still with me, you have not taken them.
They are merely rearranged.

*Grief, now I see that when you go, you leave behind
precious gems,
shooting beams of Light from deep within.
That is what I have felt bumping, breaking my shell.
I once thought it protected me from your harm,
but instead, it held me separate from your gifts.*

*Grief, always your visit leaves me with that which
I would not have known if you had not come.
I have only to let go, and all things are revealed,
for the heart that is breaking, is but opening again.*

I was not a stranger to loss or grief when I lost my husband Dwight. I wrote the above poem in 1977, about six months after my mother was killed in a head-on collision. My father had preceded her in death 5 years earlier. While my family and I were very close and my previous losses were deeply painful, nothing prepared me for the loss of my husband, my partner, my constant companion. It seeped into the smallest openings of my being and is still molding a new me even after 8 years.

This story is about my first year after my husband's passing and the way I decided to grieve… a way that was deep, heart wrenching and has served me well and helped me to heal, to keep him with me, and move on in my life in ways I would never have imagined.

It is hard to believe it has been so long since I last saw his face, watched his eyes light up when I entered the room, or felt his touch. The loss is still very present and raw sometimes, and other times it seems as if an eternity has passed. Intellectually, we can understand the dynamics of grief, the part it plays in our lives, but it shows up so differently in every person that it is impossible to actually prepare for it, even if we think we have.

Dwight and I met, ironically, in hospice. I was there to sing for his wife, who I had met about a year into her terminal diagnosis. Who could ever have imagined that the man I met that day would become my friend and, later, my husband? Dwight was known for living every moment to the fullest. One lifelong friend described him as her "Peter Pan." He was a fighter pilot, savvy entrepreneur, "celebrating artist" (as he jokingly described himself upon graduating from a prestigious art school in London after he sold his company and retired) and someone who never stopped learning. We didn't date; we just came together. Our relationship started in the middle, with no beginning. Whether traveling the world or staying at home, we were together 24/7 and we loved every minute.

I learned how to love myself more by experiencing how much he loved me. He didn't believe in Valentine's "Day" because each day was Valentine's Day to him. We showed our love for each other every day. It wasn't contrived; it was effortless.

Who would have imagined that two years after we met, he too would be diagnosed, go through agonizing, aggressive chemotherapy, and radiation, only to have the disease return two years later? Or that the next year I would say goodbye to him where we had first met, in hospice?

Perhaps his diagnosis of cancer in the second year of our relationship created an environment in which we grew closer than we would have otherwise. Or perhaps because he had lost a wife to cancer, he realized that life is fragile and sometimes short. Or maybe we were simply madly in love. I do not know why we were able to have this most amazing life together in only five years' time, I only know that we did. During our time together, I learned more from him about love, gratitude, and living to the fullest than I had learned in all the preceding years of my life.

I remember few details about the days immediately after his death – one of the blessings of grief is that, as time passes, some of the hardest parts disappear from our memories. I was numb in those early moments, and very happy for it. I do remember the desperate need I had to sit in his favorite chair, touch what he might have touched, hold his phone, put my hands on the door handles, anything I thought might still have a part of him lingering on it. I held his clothes and breathed in his scent. I wrapped myself in the sheets he had slept on. I laid my head on his pillowcase. I wore his shirts.

Confusion, forgetfulness, exhaustion, and a feeling of overwhelm became constant companions. I've always believed in a Higher Power, and this experience both deepened my belief and challenged it. I was aware that the world was going on around me, but I couldn't quite understand how to be in it. If you've ever fainted, there's a moment when the things around you take on a slow-motion, fuzzy effect. You know something is happening to you, but your conscious mind doesn't comprehend it and you can't do anything to stop it. I lived in this type of fog for months after Dwight's death. Much later, when a few of the layers of the mist had lifted, I realized how important it had been to my healing. Without that dense fog, the pain would have been impossible to bear.

Grief did not just affect my mental and emotional states; it also played out in my physical life. I broke my thumb, tripped over a gas pump, fell off a barstool, and had a myriad of aches, pains and bruises. Things that my body used to maneuver easily and automatically just didn't compute in my brain. I went for days and couldn't remember if I had eaten anything. I realized at one point that I hadn't brushed my teeth for, well, an embarrassingly long period of time. It just never crossed my mind.

In the days right after Dwight passed away, it was comforting for my best friend Suzi to stay with me. It was also important for her to return to her home in Seattle and leave me to get used to living alone again. My staying in our home, the house Dwight and I had shared, instead of selling it right away, felt safe, warm, and like a big hug from him. Sometimes I would go into the room where he last rested and sit in the quiet. I would talk to him. TUG, our puppy – named for a word Dwight coined and we said every day of our lives: It stands for "Thank U God" – always became calm when he entered that room. He was with us the night that Dwight passed away and signaled Dwight's last breath with three barks, the first time he had barked in days.

I found solace in going through Dwight's things by myself a little at a time. The first time I laughed after his death was when I cleaned out a section of his closet and moved some of my things there. He had always teased me about encroaching on his side of the closet, so after I hung my jackets in the space where his shirts once hung, I said out loud to him, "See what happens when you leave me? I take over your closet." I laughed, and then I cried.

There was no shortage of "helpful" advice, but I found one piece absolutely maddening: "Don't make any big decisions the first year." It sounds perfectly sensible and I would agree, except that there are huge decisions that have to be made during that first year: taxes – both estate and personal—family issues, jobs, possible changes in domicile, distribution of property. I needed help just doing simple things like paying bills and filing. Hiring someone to help me with all of it reduced my stress level greatly and kept me from forgetting to pay a bill and possibly having my electricity turned off.

I was both honored to have and sometimes felt burdened by advice from well-meaning friends: "Dwight loved you and he would want you to go out with friends, move on with your life, to sing again." Most of the time I barely had enough energy to get out of bed. Everything someone said to me was magnified in my heart. I felt things at a level I had never felt before. That's saying a lot, as I have been told my whole life that I am "too sensitive." I found that even people who were well meaning often said and did the most bizarre things when they encountered me. Unfortunately, I also learned that some people could be downright cold and hurtful.

About five weeks after Dwight's death, I ventured out with my step daughter-in-law to our small, local grocery store. A stranger asked her why I was crying when she saw a friend hug me. When told that my husband had just died, she walked right up and loudly announced, "Oh honey, you are young and beautiful. Don't you worry; you'll find another man in no time! I found another one in six months; I doubt it will take you two!" She seemed shocked when I burst into loud sobs.

A month later, I decided to go to a friend's birthday party. Parties or large gatherings were overwhelming for me, but I felt comfortable going to this one because I knew them well and could escape easily if I needed to. I planned to stay just long enough to say happy birthday, but not long enough for anyone to engage me in a discussion about my husband. I just wasn't ready for that yet. But, I made one miscalculation—wine. By the time I arrived, most guests were on their second or third glass. I was greeted head on with a sloppy hug and, "Oh, the last time I saw Dwight was when he won two dollars off me playing golf. He was such a great guy. I just don't understand how he could be so healthy and then…" The man went on and on before realizing I had turned away in tears. I think he was surprised that his reminiscing hadn't been a comfort to me. A year later, it would have, but not that soon. Everyone's timing is different and however long it takes, is exactly the right amount of time, no matter how much or how little time has passed.

After a particularly cruel encounter, I made the decision that I would become my own best friend, a friend like my husband had been to me, I would be good to myself, and begin to fervently guard myself from these situations. And I did. I became more proficient at excusing myself, walking across the room to get away from anything making me feel uncomfortable, or just leaving if I began to feel drained of energy. I learned to be good to myself, but hopefully still gracious to those who were merely trying to help. There is truth to the saying "humor is tragedy plus time." It took months for me to find these situations humorous, but eventually I did.

IF IT DOESN'T KILL US, IT MAKES US STRONGER

Somewhere along the way, I realized how deeply grief was touching me. I made a decision not to let the potential learning that I could get from this experience escape me. So, I began journaling my "aha" moments and discoveries. These tips are from my notes:

* I learned that I did not grieve the same way other people grieved, and that there is NO right or wrong way as long as I was being true to my feelings. I tried to allow whatever came up for me to be the thing that I handled in that moment. I had to concentrate on one thing at a time or very quickly feel overwhelmed. I could easily sink into a mound of tears, fears, and cascading emotions, and often did during the first few months.

* I learned to say no without guilt. I found out the hard way not to make long-term commitments, especially ones where I was expected to be somewhere every week at a specific time. The person I once had been, wanted to take on projects, but the person I was at the time, inside thick fog, couldn't handle it and I would end up canceling. I even gave myself permission to say no after I had first said yes.

* Crying often and deeply was cathartic. I always felt lighter and better able to handle things after I had a good cry.

* It helped to write emails rather than talk on the phone. I felt I was able to think about what I wanted to say more clearly. But I also printed a list of friends and their phone numbers. When I was sinking into pain, I could reach out to one of them easily and without having to depend on my memory.

* It was easier for me to fall asleep on the sofa and then go to bed without fully waking up. Somehow, I didn't feel as alone falling asleep in a chair instead of in a huge, empty bed.

Perhaps the biggest gift I received from Dwight and this experience of loss is a better understanding of love itself. Prior to meeting Dwight, I had associated love with hurt, eventual disappointment and control, with a few nice gestures thrown in between. Dwight taught me that love is always present, always in the forefront, always the guide that everything in life is filtered through. Love is the way to approach anything and everything. Love is present in anger, in hurt, and in argument. Love is present in friendship, in business, and in play. Love is gratitude and thoughtfulness. Love is not just the destination; its' the path to getting wherever we are looking to go. Love does not belong to just one person; it is shared between all. It can't be used up; it expands and grows. The more we love, the more we can love. As a teen, I came up with a saying, "the Love in your heart is not there to stay, love is not love till you give it away." In loving myself enough to allow the pain of loss to take me wherever it wanted, I gained a new capacity for loving and being loved. Dwight will always be my love, and if I meet another amazing man, there will be plenty of room for Dwight and for anyone that this new man has loved as well. I didn't understand that until I opened my heart to both love and pain.

Grief is not to be feared. It will turn you inside out and upside down. It will consume you if you let it, and I hope you let it. In order to build a new house, the builder sometimes has to tear down the old one. Without it, you could never become all you can be.

ABOUT THE AUTHOR

GINGER WILSON

Ginger Wilson is the child of a Midwestern college professor. She was blessed to spend three months each summer with her extended family at their rustic lake cottage in Michigan's UP. It was here that Ginger developed her deep spiritual connection with the natural world. She would later trade wilderness for the Big City by moving to Philadelphia and graduating from the Univ. of Pennsylvania. After thirty years managing her own interior design business, Ginger relocated to Sarasota where she is currently a realtor, co-authored a book on personal growth, *Through the Fire: A Woman's Guide to Transformation* and discovered Unity of Sarasota. She has one son, Jason, who is a filmmaker in Los Angeles.

SIXTEEN

Higher Love

By Ginger Wilson

After my second marriage ended in divorce, I did a lot of singing. Not because I was happy – in fact, just the opposite. I was devastated to the very depths of my being. Having spent my lifetime always seeing the glass as half-full, suddenly (and surprisingly), my glass now felt completely empty. All the joy, the lightness of spirit, and the hope that had sustained me throughout many dark days had drained from my heart. I was a hollow shell and the only emotions that I allowed to seep into me were harsh and hurtful self-recriminations: "Why didn't I do more?," "I'm worthless and unlovable," and even "Life is only filled with loss and disappointment, so what's the point of going on?"

After spending several weeks wallowing in my sadness and self-pity, I woke up one morning and noticed how beautifully the sun was shining through my bedroom skylight and dancing on my walls. I decided to pull open the curtains that had been blocking the sun and welcome the morning in. Although I am a terrible singer, I love to sing, so I told myself to think of some happy tunes and start singing every time I felt the darkness creeping back in.

The first song that came to mind, was "Oh What a Beautiful Morning" – because it WAS a magnificent morning – and somehow, I remembered every word. I sang it loudly, slightly off-key, but with true sincerity:

> *Oh, what a beautiful morning*
> *Oh, what a beautiful day*
> *I've got a beautiful feeling*
> *Everything's going my way*

How amazing! I felt a little bit better, so the next morning I decided to start the day in this same way, but this time I chose "I Can See Clearly Now." Even though I didn't *feel* the words I was singing, I desperately wanted to:

> *I can see clearly now the rain is gone*
> *I can see all obstacles in my way*
> *Gone are the dark clouds that had me blind*
> *It's gonna be a bright, bright, bright sunshiny day.*

Little by little, day by day, month by month, I started to believe the words of this song. I could actually "look all around and see nothing but blue skies." Yes, I was healing. I was starting to feel the seeds of happiness take root in my heart and was grateful to live in a world of colors again, instead of fifty shades of depressing grey.

But despite all these great strides forward, I vowed to keep on singing. One bright morning, Steve Winwood's song, "Higher Love" popped into my brain as I drew open the blinds. I couldn't remember all the lyrics, so I asked Google for some help and was perplexed and excited about what these lyrics seemed to be offering me now:

Think about it, there must be a higher love
Down in the heart or hidden in the stars above
Without it, life is wasted time
Look inside your heart, I'll look inside mine
Bring me a higher love
Bring me a higher love, oh oh
Bring me a higher love
Where's that higher love I keep thinking of?

WOW! Why had this song come to me now and what messages could I take from it? Was this my signal to start dating again? Was there a man out there as eager to find me as I was to find him? Had I spent enough time licking my wounds and was it time for me to hop back onto the saddle of the horse that had bucked me off? The problem was, I took these lyrics literally and rather than seeking a true "higher love," (such as looking within to connect with my own divine Spirit and Source), I called up my now ex-husband instead. We met that very same day, tearfully expressed our undying love for each other and within 24 hours, were back into emotional entanglement with each other again.

Despite all of the valid concerns and skepticism expressed by doubtful, but well-meaning family, friends and even our former marriage counselor, my "husband" and I threw caution to the wind and tried to put Humpty-Dumpty back together again. Unfortunately, our bliss was short-lived, because all the landmines that blasted our marriage to bits the first time around detonated again. After eighteen turbulent months, I found myself alone once again and if possible, even more devastated than before. The only thing that kept my head above water was the fact that I could no longer ask myself whether

I should have done more. I had finally swallowed the bitter pill that sometimes, no matter how much you love someone, love just isn't enough.

For the next three years, I devoted myself to healing old wounds and to finding inner balance and harmony. To do this, I first needed to face the fact that I was a relationship junkie and the only way I could break my addiction to men was by stopping cold turkey. From the time I was 15 years old, I had never lasted for more than a few months without a boyfriend or husband in my life. I was terrified at the thought of being alone! What identity did I have if not defined by a man's love? How could I survive without kisses or hugs? My withdrawal was soul-wrenchingly painful, but somehow, I managed to get by with a whole lot of help from my friends, my beloved son Jason, and my rock-solid sister Kate.

I also discovered the calm and clarity of daily meditation. Understanding the need to quiet the fearful, angry, and judgmental voices in my mind, I committed to devoting the first two hours of each day to journaling my thoughts, then releasing them through meditation. At first it felt as though I was simply going through the motions while my monkey mind continued to chatter, but gradually I found my ego dissolving into the breath. Instead of everyday thoughts bouncing around in my brain, I began to experience a sense of deep calm flowing into me with each slow inhalation and a cleansing of my soul with the release of each exhalation. Soothing colors seemed to wash over me, and glimpses of well-loved people or places would bubble up in my heart surrounded by an aura of gentle golden light. As my consciousness returned, my entire being would be filled with a profound sense of gratitude, compassion, and well-being. The world outside my window was a magnificent place and more importantly, the world I carried within was renewed and ready to take on the day. I had opened myself up to my greatest ally, my unlimited Source of love and acceptance, because I had rediscovered God.

Ever since I was child, I have always been deeply spiritual, but my connection to a Higher Power was more pagan-like than church-like. I felt God's presence most deeply in nature – the magical mystery of the changing seasons, the shifting light that dances though tree branches, the abundance, diversity and resilience of life teeming in the shallows of the lake beside our summertime cottage. We didn't go to church much after my mother died when I was six, but I loved reading the illustrated collection of *Bible Stories for Children* my aunt gave me when I was young. They had beautiful red hard-bound covers with golden embossed lettering and were filled with colorful, imaginative illustrations. My favorite stories were about the miracles Jesus performed, and as much as I wanted to believe them to be true, as I grew older, these miracles got filed away in my heart along with Cinderella's coach that turned back into a pumpkin.

However, all these dusty doubts changed back to certainty for me one sparkling September afternoon in 2018. Autumn has always been my favorite season, especially when I lived "up north" and rejoiced in the changing colors that decorated the hillsides near my Pennsylvania home. But here in Florida, I am also blessed with a magnificent giant Pink Silk-Floss tree that blossoms with a profusion of fuchsia flowers every fall.

On this particular autumn afternoon, I was on my way into the kitchen with lunch on my mind. My stomach was grumbling and I pondered what luscious leftovers awaited me in the fridge. Suddenly I was stopped in my tracks by the glorious sight outside my family room windows. A cloudless cerulean blue sky surrounded my pink-blossomed tree and the beauty took my breath away!

In this ordinary moment as I gazed up into the branches of the tree, I suddenly felt all my earthly burdens and hurtful memories falling away from me and in their place, beautiful healing recollections flowed in. Long forgotten happy times, people I had loved and lost were all there with me. It happened so quickly – in what seemed like a few heartbeats – as I felt my consciousness being transported up, up and into a place of brilliant, benevolent golden light. I was totally free – weightless – embraced by goodness in a place of pure joy…it was BLISS EUPHORIA!

It felt so familiar there – almost like coming home. I recognized a beloved presence within the center of the glowing brightness and remember saying, "So there you are!" with unbounded joy. I have no doubt that I was in the presence of God-Father-Mother-Spirit-Source. Although I can't recall actual faces or specific forms in this eternal field of light, their loving, nurturing essences are imprinted upon my soul. Time seemed to have no meaning there, but gradually I sensed my awareness being drawn back towards my earthly planet and everywhere I looked was wholeness, health, and perfection. Our natural world, all her creatures and all of humanity was in perfect balance - united in peace.

Fear lost its grasp on me as the gentle hand of eternity cradled our planet. I found myself laughing out loud – it was all so incredibly clear! Time and its terrors are only figments of our ego's imagination. The only truth is love, always there for the asking, if we only invite it to come in. This unconditional love and light are our natural state of being – our forever home. It is there waiting for all of us if we simply allow it to penetrate the barricades of doubt, division, and darkness we build around our minds and hearts.

Just as quickly as I had been lifted up, I now found myself once again standing in my mortal surroundings. My little house had never looked so welcoming or filled with love before. As I gazed around at my time-worn furniture and belongings, I seemed to be seeing them with different eyes. What had appeared so mundane just moments before, was now suffused with a beauty untarnished by time. My physical body, too, felt completely revitalized, as if reborn. Washed free of life's worries, innocence blossomed in my being and filled me with a deep and grounded certainty that what I had just experienced was the truest experience of my lifetime. I didn't "believe" this to be true; I "knew" it to be so.

Ever since that unforgettable afternoon in September, I have been asking myself what exactly happened that day and why did it happen to ME? The miracle moment I experienced could be likened to what others have described as a "near-death experience," but instead of getting this glimpse of eternity on death's doorstep, I was granted a surprise sneak peek while still perfectly healthy and alive. Perhaps this gift came to me because I had finally quit looking outside of myself for love and instead, chose to search my own heart. By letting go of my constant need for outer validation, in the quiet of meditation I was able to find my own self-worth through the unconditional love of God. By forgiving others, but more importantly myself, and living in gratitude for all the lessons I had learned along the way, I was opening myself up to the greatest love of all – my partnership with my True Self and God.

Some say it takes a leap of faith to believe in a power greater than ourselves. How small is that notion when within each person, plant and creature lies eternity – the blinding magnificence of everything? I also understand that this miraculous holy moment I experienced –

this euphoric bliss consciousness is available to ALL of us! I am no one special or uniquely chosen to receive this gift, since all it takes for anyone to receive this miracle is to simply open up to God that lives within and all around us.

I now know that this human construct we call our "life" is but a tiny filament of the endless energetic web that connects us to the Divine and to each other. Love and unity are the truths that will heal our planet and embraced by this certainty, I am forever changed. My deepest desire going forward for the rest of my time here on Earth is to share this good news– this en"light"enment – with all those willing to be set free.

It is our birthright. It is our grace.

And, at last, I have found that Higher Love I'd been thinking of…

Notes:

ABOUT THE AUTHOR

Laurel D. Rund

Laurel D. Rund is a published author and digital artist. Her creative journey began at 64, after the death of her husband of 42 years. Laurel's words and art are the *Essence of Laurel*. Her 'Art from the Heart' is often described as unique, inspirational and moving.

Laurel spent 30 years in management in corporate America. She has two sons and four grandchildren. Laurel remarried several years ago and is delighted that she found room in her heart to experience love once more. Laurel's spiritual journey is transformative as she explores her soul's purpose.

SEVENTEEN

The Gift of Aging

By Laurel D. Rund

As I reach another milestone in life – my 75th birthday - aging with grace and purpose is foremost in my mind. It is profound to know that there is more of my life's journey behind me than in front of me. Aging comes with an understanding that time does not stand still, it keeps moving forward. Although I must say, during this pandemic of Covid-19, it feels as if time has been grinding and halting – moving forward with resistance. The unknown looms, and the social fabric of our lives has been changed for years to come.

But I digress. As a gift to myself just before my 70th birthday, I attended the Hay House Orlando "I Can Do It" conference. For me, it was a meaningful and inspirational time, which included a poignant memorial service for Dr. Wayne Dyer who had just passed away – he was scheduled to be the opening night keynote speaker.

I wanted to write about one particular experience I had at the conference for quite some time, but felt stuck, unable to put into words a description of my transformative soul retrieval journey led by renowned Shaman, Dr. Alberto Villoldo, Ph.D.

As the session began, the Shaman told the participants that a soul retrieval journey is a time where one enters a sacred space to heal the past and chart a new destiny. I felt like an open vessel ready to travel to the unknown.

After conducting rituals with the audience, it was time for all of us to quiet down and go into a meditative state. With my eyes closed, his mesmerizing guided meditation led me to a path in the woods, where at the entry of the path, I was told that a power animal would meet me.

A large buck greeted me, and as I focused my eyes on this strong, superb animal – it suddenly morphed into a hawk that spread its wings and guided me through the woods to a clearing.

The Shaman asked me to sit down on a rock in the center of the clearing and wait. He said that a spirit would appear behind me, and at some point, I would feel its presence. I suddenly got goose bumps and knew it was time to turn around and greet this mysterious entity.

Upon turning, I saw an elderly Native American woman with braids standing behind me. Her beautiful face radiated with kindness, her skin was crinkled and aged, her eyes were engaging and caring, and she presented me with a gentle and enchanting smile. Her loving energy encircled me and opened my heart. I reached over and felt compelled to trace my fingers across the deep wrinkles on her face and around her eyes. I felt like the lines were tracing a map of this extraordinary being. We spent some time basking in each other's energy in some kind of energetic force field. The Shaman's voice broke through and guided me to walk away with the spirit by my side - to return home through the forest path which led me to the clearing.

But, before leaving the forest, he directed me on my soul retrieval journey, to transmute and absorb my power animals (the buck, the hawk) and the spirit into my being. Almost immediately, I felt the power animals and the Wise Old Woman morph into my human form and soul. As guided to do, I left the forest and was transported back to the present moment – my soul retrieval was completed. At that time, I felt peaceful and calm, and wondered "what did this all mean?" My intuition kicked in and told me that I had retrieved my "wise old woman" (my WOW) as a lesson about recognizing the strength, wisdom, gentleness, and grace that lies within me. It was all about honoring my age.

When I returned home from the conference, there was urgency within me to recreate an image of what I had seen, and then to write about the experience. The soul retrieval journey was emblazoned in my head and heart. It had set a path of acceptance and joy for me as I stepped into my seventh decade with gratitude and a newfound sense of anticipation.

I felt exhilarated when I was able to envision and create a piece of art which represented what I saw during my soul retrieval journey. My Woman of Wisdom artwork hangs on a wall in my house. When it catches my eye, it also catches my essence because it reminds me of my soul journey experience.

The writing of the story was more challenging. When I tried to find the words to describe my journey, I felt blocked. Somehow, deep within me, I knew that there was an unknown purpose for this story and that I needed to be patient until it revealed itself to me.

The Universe would let me know when it was time to write my story, just as it had guided me to create a piece of art which would serve as a visual reminder of that exquisite experience. Woman of Wisdom – Laurel Rund

The Epiphany

One morning, about three months after the conference, while driving my car through an area that is populated with lush moss-filled oak trees, I had an epiphany. I slowed my car – as I always do when passing under the arch of these glorious trees – and greeted them tenderly with "hello trees!" There is something about this particular street that has always "talked to me." I never fail to purposefully slow my car and greet the trees, taking time to be present with them and to honor their magnificence. It always leaves me with a sense of peacefulness and gratitude. It makes my heart feel good. It's actually a meditative moment in time.

As I drove on, I began to think about the dichotomy between how we see trees and how we see our elders. The purpose of the soul retrieval journey finally percolated up; it literally showed itself to me when I stopped to greet the trees. My writing block was lifted!

When we pass a tree that has become glorious in its old age, we look at that tree in awe as we revere its strength and beauty whether or not its bark is missing or cracked, or its branches broken off.

Here's the epiphany - I believe we humans are very much like trees. We show our age with wrinkles, changes in our bodies and its imperfections. And yet, as we grow older, we, too, have a community to build and a story to share. Our culture, however, has often stated that when people get older, they are "past their prime" and become invisible. Maybe it makes some people uncomfortable with their own aging process, or maybe heartlessness has replaced caring.

"Trees are sanctuaries. Whoever knows how to speak to them, whoever knows how to listen to them, can learn the truth. They do not preach learning and precepts, they preach, undeterred by particulars, the ancient law of life." Hermann Hesse

It's interesting how many people have come to love and honor trees. I know several devoted tree huggers. People have sat in trees for months to protect them from destruction. As they get older, trees reach across to each other and their branches touch – intertwine. They share their energy, their power and offer a place for humans to be shaded and rest under their glorious limbs. They build a community. And there are many stories held within each tree – what it encountered as it grew into maturity.

I created a piece of artwork called Elegy to a Tree in 2009 during a time of grief and loss in my life. My husband had passed away a few months before. I turned to the creative arts to help me cope with my grief and was given an art assignment where I was to go outside to draw a tree. To my dismay, one of my favorite trees had been taken down. I was in shock – it was another loss. Even back then, I was seeing the way trees and people mirror one another's existence. Here is my artwork and poem, Strength and Glory – Elegy to a Tree

Elegy to a Tree – Laurel Rund
Strength and Glory ~ Elegy to a Tree

Welcoming all to a vision of grandeur, you stood tall and proud
with your trunk rooted firmly into the ground.
As your limbs reached towards the heavens, I watched in awe
as playful birds rested on your bare branches and marveled
when your sparse limbs were illuminated by gleaming sunbeams.

You withstood the force of fierce winds, unrestrained rainstorms
and seemed to revel as lightning danced raggedly around you.
During your time on Earth, your spirit was one of
beauty, dignity, grace and, above all, courage.

Then, suddenly one day you disappeared!
Thoughtlessly cut down to fulfill man's need for youthful perfection,
you were replaced with a rather unremarkable seedling.
Was it time for your journey to come to an end
so that a new life could begin?
A reminder of one's mortality ~ your loss was jarring!

Please know, oh grand tree, that
the image of your magnificent strength and glory
will forever have an honored place within my soul.

There are many lessons to be shared and taught by our elders. Our society all too often disregards the journeys and stories of the aged and places its attention on youthfulness. Yes, life is about hope, youth and building a life, but it is also about the wisdom one has gained throughout the years. It's about our strength and glory.

Gabriel Garci-a-Marquez, author of "Love in the Time of Cholera" said about the essence of aging: "Age has no reality except in the physical world. The essence of a human being is resistant to the passage of time. Our inner lives are eternal, which is to say that our spirits remain as youthful and vigorous as when we were in full bloom."

Being an elder, a Woman of Wisdom, a WOW, has given me a new perspective about aging. I've learned that what I feel about the outside of my human form as it ages has nothing to do with the date of my birth. Because you see - my spiritual being is ageless, it came with me the day I was born and will transform with me when I leave my earthly body behind.

Just like my gray hair, wrinkles, aches and pains, my life is filled with joy, growth, challenges, heartaches, and bumps in the road. These are the things that build character, wisdom, and courage. This is how I can learn and grow and find my purpose.

"In the winter of our lives, we become stripped down to our essence like a tree. We may become more radiant than ever at this stage because our inner light shines brighter through our eyes as time passes. Beauty at this age comes from the very core of our being – our essence. This essence is a reminder that there is nothing to fear in growing older and that there is a kind of beauty that comes only after one has spent many years on earth." Madison Taylor

I have learned to honor and treasure all the decades of my life, very much like the rings within the trunk of a tree which represent and record its timeline.

Today, go hug a tree. Then go and talk with and hug an Elder. Recognize the gifts they have within them and stories they must impart. Then you will experience the gifts of aging beings!

"Beautiful young people are accidents of nature, but beautiful old people are works of art." Eleanor Roosevelt. So, what is the gift of aging? Knowing that I am a work of art inside and out! I am infinite!

Namaste, Laurel Diane Rund